MRS TINNE'S WARDROBE

A Liverpool Lady's Clothes, 1900-1940

For Dr Alexine Tinne (1923-2011)
With grateful thanks

© National Museums Liverpool 2012

Published by The Bluecoat Press, Liverpool
Book design by March Graphic Design Studio, Liverpool
Printed by Latitude Press

Front cover: Detail Cat. no. 103.
Back cover: Cat. no. 135, Cat. no. 172.
Title page: Cat. no. 116.

ISBN 978-1-902700-48-9

MRS TINNE'S WARDROBE

A Liverpool Lady's Clothes, 1900-1940

Pauline Rushton

CONTENTS

INTRODUCTION 6

EMILY MARGARET TINNE (1886-1966) AND THE TINNE FAMILY OF LIVERPOOL 9

SHOPPING IN LIVERPOOL, 1910-1940 17

THE TINNE COLLECTION OF CLOTHING 27

SELECTIVE CATALOGUE OF THE COLLECTION

DAY CLOTHES 36

EVENING CLOTHES 50

OUTDOOR CLOTHES AND FURS 62

BLOUSES 80

UNDERWEAR 90

BATHING COSTUMES 100

SHOES 104

HATS 112

ACCESSORIES 130

BABIES' AND CHILDREN'S CLOTHES 146

APPENDIX

INVENTORY OF THE TINNE COLLECTION 172

GLOSSARY OF TERMS 187

SELECT BIBLIOGRAPHY 191

INTRODUCTION

The Tinnes of Liverpool were, and are, a remarkable family. During the nineteenth and early twentieth centuries, they were one of Liverpool's most successful merchant families, as part of Sandbach, Tinne & Co., yet they remain one of the least well-known. They lived quietly in Liverpool's southern suburb of Aigburth, among many of the city's other great merchant families whose names are, perhaps, better known to history. By contrast, their lifestyle was relatively modest and they avoided outward display, despite their considerable wealth. Nevertheless, the Tinnes counted several fascinating characters amongst their number, not least one of the earliest women explorers of Africa.[1] Sadly, a lack of space here prevents me from doing full justice to the history of the family, although I have given a brief outline of parts of it in the introductory essay.

This book concerns one who was not a Tinne by birth, but who married into their ranks – Emily Margaret McCulloch, the Mrs Tinne of the title. Quite unintentionally, by means of the huge collection of clothes that she amassed, and which now belongs to the National Museums Liverpool, she has made her own, unique contribution to the history of the Tinne family. Her wardrobe provides us with a snap-shot of changing fashions, as worn by a middle-class woman in one of Britain's great cities, in the period between the two World Wars. It also tells us something about how people shopped for clothes in Liverpool during that time.

The Collection's greatest value lies in its mixture of the mundane and the extraordinary. Many museum collections of garments from this period tend mainly to represent fashionable dress and clothes kept for special occasions such as weddings. In contrast, in the Tinne collection, one can see a broad range of clothes worn by one person every day and over a long period of time. In addition, a large number of Emily's children's clothes are also preserved.

This selective Catalogue of the Collection is divided into chapters by type of garment. In each one, the best-preserved and most representative examples of their kind are described and illustrated. A full inventory of the entire Collection appears in the Appendix at the end of the Catalogue, arranged once again by garment-type and listed in museum number-order. A Glossary of the textile terms used in the Catalogue entries may also be found in the Appendix.

This book might never have been written had it not been for the unfailing help and support of one person in particular – Emily Tinne's youngest daughter, Dr Alexine Tinne. Not only was she extremely generous in donating the Collection to the National Museums Liverpool, but, over many years, she patiently responded to all my questions about her parents and siblings, and supplied me with a wealth of original documents and family photographs, many of which appear here. I am deeply indebted to her for all her assistance, encouragement and kindness.

I am also grateful to the late John Ernest Tinne, Alexine's brother, for the use of his unpublished family history, *The Story of the Tinne Family*, which I found an invaluable and highly amusing source of information about the Tinnes. It reinforced my view that they deserve to be more widely known.

My thanks also go to a number of professional colleagues who have helped with this book. Anthea Jarvis, former Principal Curator at the Gallery of Costume, Manchester Art Galleries, and my predecessor as Curator of Costume at Liverpool, was responsible for acquiring the major part of the Tinne Collection in 1966-67. She very kindly examined and gave me her opinion on several items in the Collection about which I had queries. Annie Lord and Anne-Marie Hughes, former Textile Conservators at NML, carried out a programme of conservation on many of the garments, over several years, before they were photographed. Sue Barker, former Metals Conservator, cleaned the metal accessories. David Flower, NML's Senior Photographer, was responsible for the excellent photographs. Tony Parker, Assistant Curator of Vertebrates, identified some of the feathers included in the Collection. Anne Gleave, Curator of Photographic Archives, gave me help and guidance in selecting some of the photographs of Liverpool shops which are featured here. David Govier, former Curator of Maritime Archives (temporary) gave me help with, and access to the Tinne papers in the Bryson Collection at the Merseyside Maritime Museum. Robin Emmerson, former Curator of Decorative Art and Alyson Pollard, Curator of Metalwork and Glass, read the draft texts and made many helpful suggestions.

I am grateful also to Colin Wilkinson at The Bluecoat Press and to Michael March at March Graphic Design Studio for their skilful production of the book.

Pauline Rushton
Curator of Costume and Textiles
National Museums Liverpool

EMILY MARGARET TINNE (1886-1966) AND THE TINNE FAMILY OF LIVERPOOL

Most of the garments in this collection were owned and worn by Emily Margaret Tinne. She was born Emily Margaret McCulloch on 21 August 1886 near Calcutta, where her father, a Presbyterian minister, the Reverend William McCulloch, was the principal of a theological college at Chinsurah, West Bengal. Details of Emily's early life are not entirely clear but she spent her first years in India before being sent home to England at about the age of seven, in 1893, to a boarding school for the daughters of the clergy, in Sevenoaks, Kent. Her main carer was her mother's sister, Emily Patterson, and during school holidays she and her two brothers and sister lived with their aunt Emily and their Patterson grandparents in Edinburgh. Her parents did not return to Edinburgh from India until the early 1920s.

In about 1904, at the age of 18, Emily began to train as a domestic science teacher at the well-known Edinburgh School of Cookery (now the Edinburgh College of Domestic Science) in Atholl Crescent.

Upon completion of her training, in about 1906, Emily and her aunt moved to Liverpool to live with her uncle, her mother's brother, William Brogden Patterson. He was a well-established surgeon and a patron of the arts, who lived in a spacious house in Aigburth, a prosperous southern suburb of Liverpool. The house, at 1 Aigburth Hall Road, remains there today and looks much the same as it probably did in Emily's day.

Emily's first job was as a teacher at the Liverpool Training School of Cookery & Technical College of Domestic Science, in Colquitt Street, Liverpool. It was while she was living with her uncle that Emily met her future husband, Dr Philip Frederic Tinne, a local GP. Exactly how they met is not recorded, nor indeed remembered by the family. It could have been socially, as neighbours, since Philip lived in nearby Mayfield Road at that time, or perhaps it was due to the mutual contacts between Philip and Emily's uncle in the world of medicine. It may even have been at the 1906 wedding of Philip's younger brother, John A. Tinne, to Katherine Mackay, at which Emily, a friend of the bride, acted as bridesmaid.[2] Whatever the circumstances, we do know that by 1909 Emily and Philip had become engaged. They married on 14 July 1910 at the Presbyterian Church, Toxteth Park, Liverpool. They honeymooned in Ireland, probably at Culdaff, County Donegal, where they stayed in the house owned by Philip's father, John Ernest Tinne. This later became the setting for many happy family holidays.

Emily and Philip Tinne on their wedding day, 14 July 1910.

Opposite: Emily Margaret Tinne, possibly taken during her honeymoon in 1910.

John Abraham Tinne (1807-1884).

The Tinnes were Dutch sugar merchants and ship-owners. They first came to Liverpool in 1813 from Demerara, in what was then Dutch Guiana, later to be re-named British Guiana (and finally, following independence in 1966, Guyana) on the North East coast of South America. During the eighteenth century, the Dutch, using their experience in constructing dykes, had reclaimed the land around the Demerara River, near the capital Georgetown, for sugar plantations, using slave labour. They also produced coffee, cotton, rum and tropical hardwoods.

Philip Frederic Tinne, the first Tinne to settle in Liverpool, was born in The Hague in 1772. He worked for several years in the Netherlands Diplomatic Service in London, before moving back to Holland in 1793. In 1796, following Napoleon's occupation of Holland, he went out to Dutch Guiana, where his cousin Matthieu Tinne was Collector of Taxes. There he built up a lucrative career as an administrator, becoming Secretary of the colony by 1801, and wealthy enough to buy a coffee plantation, named Vauxhall and Westminster. In 1810, still unable to return home to the Netherlands due to the continued French occupation, he and his Scottish-born wife, Anna Rose, travelled to England and then Scotland, where they spent some time in Greenock. Here he met James McInroy, who in 1782 had set up in business as a sugar merchant in Demerara. In 1790 he was joined in the venture by Samual Sandbach, Charles Stewart Parker and George Robertson. Their business involved the import of sugar, molasses, coffee and rum from Demerara, but they also dealt in 'prime Gold Coast Negroes'[3], and used them to work their plantations there.

In 1813, the same year that Demerara became a British Colony, Philip Tinne went into partnership with McInroy, agreeing to be based at the company's Liverpool branch, along with Samuel Sandbach. That part of the company was then re-named Sandbach, Tinne & Co., the name under which the firm was to trade until its eventual closure in 1966. McInroy, Sandbach & Co. continued to run the other part of the business from Demerara, and briefly, from Glasgow as McInroy, Parker & Co.

Philip Tinne took a house in Liverpool at 6 St Anne Street, Everton Brow, and was joined in June 1813 by his wife Anna Rose and their two sons, John Abraham, aged five, and William Thomas, aged three. They subsequently lived at numbers 27 and 29 St Anne Street, before moving out to Aigburth, probably during the 1830s when many other merchant families were also leaving the city centre for the greener suburbs.

Besides growing coffee, Sandbach, Tinne & Co. acquired several sugar plantations in Demerara, the first two being Diamond and Providence. Other properties included the estates known as Wales, Industry, Greenveld and Leonora. Sandbach, Tinne & Co. prospered, receiving an extra financial boost of about £100,000 in 1835 (some £7.6 million in modern terms) as compensation from the British government for giving up their slaves on the plantations. Following the 1834 emancipation of the slaves, Demerara's sugar estates were worked by a combination of indentured Chinese and Indian labour and by former slaves who continued as paid labourers.[4] When he died in Holland in 1844, Philip Tinne left some £40,000 in his will, the equivalent in today's money of about £3.1 million.[5]

Philip's younger son, William Tinne, died unmarried, following a career as a captain in the 8th

John Ernest Tinne (1845-1925).

Left Clayton Lodge, Aigburth, Liverpool, about 1920-30.

King's Royal Irish Hussars, but his older brother John Abraham followed their father into the Demarara sugar trade. He kept detailed accounts of his growing fortune, with property in The Hague and in Liverpool. He became a J.P. and Deputy Lord Lieutenant for the County of Lancashire. Aigburth, where he lived, although a somewhat isolated suburb in the early nineteenth century, was gradually to become one of the city's most prosperous areas. It was populated by many of Liverpool's wealthiest ship-owning families, cotton brokers and those engaged in the legal professions and medicine; families, in other words, who were very similar to the Tinnes.

John Abraham Tinne lived for most of his life, until his death in 1884, at *Briarley,* a large colonial-style house built by the family on Aigburth Road, about half a mile from the River Mersey and some five or six miles from the city centre. *Briarley* was set in its own extensive grounds, with sandstone stables and piggeries and even a purpose-built camellia house for

growing exotic flowers. But in 1884, following a set back in the family's fortunes on the sugar futures market, they were forced to move out of *Briarley* when its upkeep proved too expensive. They moved into another house, *Mostyn,* which was still spacious but smaller than *Briarley*, built in its grounds. The main house was eventually demolished and the land sold off to Liverpool Corporation. From 1910 onwards, new streets and houses were laid out on the area it had once occupied.

When John Abraham died in 1884 he left a very detailed inventory[6] of the *Briarley* estate, itemising every object, even down to the individual plants in the greenhouses, and, more importantly, the then enormous sum of £121, 586. In today's money, this is the equivalent of some £9.8 million.[7] Most of this money was, no doubt, generated by the family's sugar estates, which, by the 1880s, were producing some 30,000 tons of sugar annually,[8] but equally, their shipping business was extremely lucrative. In the early years, they had only two ships of their own, the *Sandbach*, built in 1828, and the *Demerara,* built in 1829, and consequently were forced to charter ships from other owners. But from the 1860s onwards, Sandbach Tinne & Co. built up a fleet of some 32 sailing ships. They carried indentured Indian and Chinese labourers from Calcutta to Demerara, and cargoes of tea and European passengers to and from the Far East, as well as the cargoes of sugar, rum and molasses.

John Abraham Tinne and his wife Margaret Sandbach, daughter of Samuel Sandbach, had ten children. Their seventh child and third son, John Ernest Tinne, was born in 1845 and also followed his father into the sugar business.

In 1874, John Ernest Tinne married Deborah Wainwright, daughter of the Mayor of Port of Spain, Trinidad, and in December of that year their son, another Philip Frederic Tinne, Emily's future husband, was born in Georgetown, British Guiana. Philip spent his early years living at his grandfather's home, *Briarley*, and then, after 1884, at *Mostyn*. He went to Eton at the age of 13, in 1888, and was there until 1892. He was then educated at Magdalen College, Oxford, taking his

B.A. in 1896 and gaining a Third in Physiology in 1897. While at Oxford he developed an ambition to study for a career as a curator at London's South Kensington Museum, now the Victoria and Albert Museum, but his father encouraged him instead to pursue a more lucrative career as a doctor, the family fortunes having suffered further set backs by this time. It was generally felt that Philip's father, John Ernest, was not quite as able a businessman as his own father, John Abraham, had been. Consequently, between 1897 and 1902 Philip Tinne trained at St George's Hospital, London, finally working there as a House Surgeon and Physician in 1903-04.

Upon leaving St George's, Philip Tinne went on to serve for several years as a ship's surgeon with the Elder Dempster line,[9] before returning to Liverpool in 1907 to set up his practice as a GP at 4 Mayfield Road, Aigburth.

Following their marriage, Emily and Philip's first family home was *Oak Cottage,* at 6 The Serpentine, off Aigburth Road, where they lived between 1910 and 1923. They then moved to a much larger property, *Clayton Lodge*, at 32 Aigburth Road, where they were to remain for the rest of their lives. Here they brought up their six children, and here Philip Tinne had his surgery, built on to the back of the ground floor of the house. Probably built in the 1840s, *Clayton Lodge* was a house in its own right and not the lodge belonging to a grander mansion, as its name would suggest. It stood in some three acres of gardens and occupied the site of an earlier, possibly late eighteenth-century farmhouse, the remains of which, in the form of slate troughs, still survived in the *Lodge's* cellars. The house remained in the family's possession until 1969, when, becoming too expensive to maintain, it was sold to property developers with planning permission for the building of up to eight houses on its land. But the houses were never built and the *Lodge* passed through the hands of several other owners before being demolished. Only in 2002 were houses finally built on the site.

While living at *Clayton Lodge*, Philip Tinne became a widely respected and much-loved family doctor among the residents of the neighbouring areas of Aigburth and Garston, practising for

Helen Tinne, posing for one of Miss Watts' theatrical productions, about 1933-34.

Right: Elspeth Deborah (1911-2000) with her nanny (name now unknown).

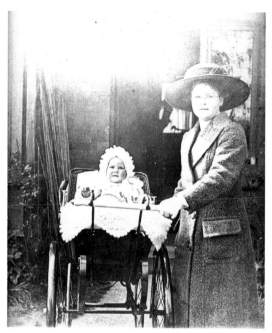

some 50 years.[10] During World War I he took charge of Crofton Recovery Hospital, Aigburth, and during World War II he organised Garston's Sir Alfred Jones Memorial Hospital as a first-aid unit for casualties.[11] While Aigburth was known then as a wealthy suburb, Garston was populated by some of the city's less well-off citizens, and family memory has it that, during the Depression in the late 1920s and early 1930s, Philip would often accept payment in kind for his services from local shopkeepers, in lieu of cash. This was at a time, of course, before the arrival of the National Health Service, when one paid one's doctor for individual visits, and poorer patients avoided seeing a doctor unless it was absolutely necessary. A former patient of Dr Tinne's remembers that, in the 1930s, home visits cost seven shillings and sixpence but the fee was less if one could attend the surgery in person.[12]

When Philip's father, John Ernest Tinne, died in 1925, despite his alleged shortcomings as a businessman, he too left a substantial amount of money in his will; £161,830, worth some £7.1 million in today's money.[13] Once all his other bequests were paid, this sum was divided equally between John Ernest's four surviving sons, including Philip, and invested for them by their Trustees so that they could each draw an income from it. It accounts for the lifestyle that he and his family were able to adopt, one that would have been beyond the financial means of most ordinary family doctors in the 1920s and 1930s.

The Tinne children enjoyed a comfortable, typically middle-class upbringing in the period between the two World Wars. The eldest child, born on 3 May 1911, while Emily and Philip lived at Oak Cottage, was Elspeth Deborah Tinne. She was followed by John Ernest on 7 November 1913, and Bertha Emily on 22 February 1916. The fourth child, Philip, born in 1917, tragically died of whooping cough in infancy, as did so many children at that time. He was followed by Helen

Margaret Tinne, born on 30 January 1919. Alexine Tinne arrived on 19 July 1923, and the youngest child, Philip William Labart Tinne, known as Pip, was born on 21 November 1929, by which time the family had moved to *Clayton Lodge*.

Like their father before them, both boys, John Ernest (known in the family as Ernest) and Pip, were educated at Eton, Ernest between 1927 and 1931, and Pip for one year, 1943-44, following a period at preparatory school in Shrewsbury. Pip completed his education at Liverpool College, Mossley Hill, near Liverpool.

The girls were educated at local schools, Elspeth and Bertha at Liverpool College, Huyton, and Helen and Alexine at Belvedere School, Princes Park, Liverpool, part of the Girls' Public Day School Trust.

The girls also regularly attended the dancing classes offered by many middle-class ladies during the 1920s and 1930s, notably those run by a Miss Watt in Edge Lane, near the city centre, and, nearer home, by the Misses Rosser at 23 Western Drive, Grassendale, off Aigburth Road. Alexine Tinne recalled that, of the two, the lessons of the Rosser sisters were the more serious, leading to dancing certificates, while Miss Watts' lessons were more entertaining, giving them the opportunity to dress up in costume and perform at dancing displays, musical revues and pantomimes. Some of these were held at the Crane Theatre, now the Epstein Theatre, in Hanover Street, Liverpool.

Alexine Tinne remembered that, when she was a child during the 1920s, the family usually had at least seven servants. They included a cook, a butler, two housemaids, a nanny and an assistant nanny, and a gardener. Some of the servants' work clothes survive in the Collection and family recollections of them persist. Alexine Tinne was told by older family members that, in the period just before her birth, the family's cook was an Irish Catholic woman named Mary, who had formerly worked for the Tinnes at *Mostyn*. The kitchen maid was Rebecca, a Protestant, and she and Mary often had heated exchanges in the kitchen, delaying the arrival of dinner on the table on more than one occasion. Such incidents would not have been uncommon, one imagines, in a city such as Liverpool in the 1920s when the sectarian divide was still strongly felt by many people.

The butler at this time was a Mr Brown and his wife succeeded Mary as cook at *Clayton Lodge* in 1923, the year of Alexine's birth, so presumably working relationships in the kitchen improved around then.

The servants had separate accommodation in the form of a cottage, with kitchen, scullery and three bedrooms, situated over what were originally the stables at *Clayton Lodge*, and which later became a garage. In the 1930s, the servants were much reduced in number, both because of the expense of keeping so many, and also possibly due to recruitment difficulties, with fewer people willing to enter domestic service by that time. Consequently, their accommodation became vacant while the remaining few presumably 'lived out' nearby. This was fortunate in one sense in that the vacated premises were then used by Emily to store part of her ever-growing wardrobe of clothes.

Philip and Emily Tinne, in the background, at the wedding of their daughter Helen to Gordon Orry, 10 April 1948, at St Anne's Church, Aigburth, Liverpool. The bride wears her mother's wedding dress from 1910. All Tinne family photographs are reproduced courtesy of Dr Alexine Tinne.

SHOPPING FOR CLOTHES IN LIVERPOOL
1910-1940

For those who could afford it, shopping for clothes in Liverpool in the period between the two World Wars must have been an exciting experience, such was the choice and variety available in Britain's greatest seaport. It was also a period of transition, with gradual change taking place in the 'pecking order' of garment retailers in particular. The most prestigious shops, providing an exclusive made-to-measure service, were still located in Bold Street, known during the late nineteenth and early twentieth centuries as the 'Bond Street of the North'. Chief among these were Cripps, Sons & Co., T. & S. Bacon and De Jong et Cie who, from as early as the 1860s onwards, had catered for the county gentry and the mercantile elite, known as 'the carriage trade', at the top end of the social scale. Their customers included the wives and daughters of wealthy local shipowners and cottonbrokers.

After the Bold Street shops came the large department stores, headed by the biggest, George Henry Lee & Co. Ltd in Basnett Street, and followed by the Bon Marché in Church Street, Owen Owen Ltd in London Road and Lewis's in Ranelagh Street. Lee's customers included the families of businessmen and members of the professions, such as doctors and solicitors, while both Owen Owen's and Lewis's catered for the needs of the lower middle and working-classes. At the beginning of the twentieth century Lee's still manufactured their garments themselves in workshops located over their premises, which made them quite expensive and placed them out of the reach of many people. But, gradually, as the department stores began to stock more reasonably priced ready-made garments, the better-off working-class families could afford to shop at places like the Bon Marché and Lewis's. Such clothes were often supplied to the retailers by local makers, based in factories which had sprung up in several parts of the city from about 1900 onwards to supply the ready-made trade.

Emily Tinne patronised both the Bold Street shops and the department stores, and, like other women of her social class, she also had many of her clothes made for her by a local dressmaker, a Mrs Taylor, the wife of a neighbouring chauffeur, George Taylor.[14] The Tinne Collection still includes lengths of fabric, mainly plain and devoré silk velvets, which were obviously left over from the making of garments by Mrs Taylor (see Appendix, Inventory, Miscellaneous).

From Cripps' Emily seems to have bought mainly hats and coats, the sorts of things that one would not have had made by a local dressmaker or milliner. The coats include four high quality examples in wool, trimmed with rabbit or beaver fur (including Cat. nos. 49 and 51) and an expensive-looking one in silk ottoman trimmed with moleskin (Cat. no. 55). There is also a

Owen Owen Ltd, Clayton Square, about 1934. *National Museums Liverpool (Merseyside Maritime Museum, Stewart Bale Archive).*

Cripps in the 1970s shortly before it ceased trading.

beautiful and unusual evening cape in black silk crepe trimmed with ruffles of black silk satin ribbon (Cat. no. 63). The hats include a number of very stylish cloche hats which were popular in the late 1920s and early 1930s (Cat. nos. 164, 168-172). The quality of these items is typical of clothes made or sold by Cripps, who were considered one of the top clothing retailers in Bold Street.

Founded at number 48 Bold Street in 1836 by John Cripps, a shawl merchant and manufacturer and importer of ladies' mantles, the business grew steadily. In 1849 Cripps moved to 12 and 14 Bold Street, expanding still further in 1854 to accommodate a silk department, and in 1856 a department for 'ladies dresses, both British and foreign, and a department for mourning requisites and dress making'.[15] By 1861, Fraser's *Guide to Liverpool* noted that 'the new premises, by their extent, tasteful arrangements and decorations, are ornamental even in this town of commercial palaces'.[16] In 1867, advertisements for Cripps made it clear that they were also able to offer their customers a bespoke dressmaking service, provided by dressmakers based on the premises, in Cripps' own workrooms.[17] This was to be the pattern adopted by the other high-class ladies outfitters in Bold Street and by George Henry Lee & Co. Ltd in Basnett Street. By the early 1900s, Cripps employed some 200 staff. By the 1920s, they also had a large fur department, where Emily Tinne bought her coats.

The Collection includes no examples of garments from either of the other two major Bold Street retailers, T. & S. Bacon and De Jong et Cie, indicating perhaps that Emily did not patronise them. This may be because they were too expensive, particularly Bacon's, and were out of even her price range.

Church Street, Liverpool.

Advertising pamphlet published to celebrate the 75th birthday of George Henry Lee & Co. Ltd, 1928. *National Museums Liverpool.*

Left: Church Street, Liverpool, about 1930.

Judging by surviving marked garments in the Collection, Emily's favourite department stores were George Henry Lee's, the Bon Marché, Owen Owen's and Lewis's. There were others that she may have patronised, including Henderson's and C & A Modes in Church Street, but there are no surviving garments from either of these establishments in the Collection so one cannot be sure. She may also have shopped at Blackler's Stores in Elliot Street and Great Charlotte Street, judging by the blouse and the swimwear in the Collection marked with the *St Margaret* trademark (including Cat. no. 92). Blackler's claimed to be the only Liverpool supplier of garments bearing this brand name. They were made by N. Corah & Sons Ltd, at their St Margaret's Works in Leicester, where they specialised in the manufacture of women's and children's woollen and silk underwear, hosiery and other garments.

George Henry Lee & Co. Ltd was founded by the brothers George and Henry Boswell Lee in 1853 as a Straw Bonnet Warehouse at 12 Basnett Street, Liverpool. By 1857, George Henry Lee and Henry Boswell Lee Jnr, sons of the first Henry Boswell Lee, are recorded in the local street directories as general warehousemen, trading in Basnett Street. In 1858 Thomas Oakshott joined the staff, which by then consisted of thirteen employees selling lace, silks and household goods. In 1861, Henry Boswell Lee retired early and left his brother in charge of the business. In the same year, George Henry Lee took Thomas Oakshott into partnership with him. They ran Lee's together until 1874, when George Henry himself retired to pursue other interests, leaving Oakshott in sole control.

The business expanded rapidly during the 1870s and 1880s, so that by the end of the century they owned numbers 24-36 Basnett Street, as well as 25-27 Leigh Street. In 1887, Oakshott made local history by becoming the first tradesman to be elected Mayor of Liverpool.

In 1897, the firm became a Limited Company, with all the shares in the business held by the Oakshott family, although it was still known as George Henry Lee & Co. Ltd. Thomas Oakshott died in 1910, leaving the store with some 1,200 employees. In 1919, the firm was bought by Gordon Selfridge of London, a pioneer of the department store, as one of his first provincial stores.

In 1940, Lee's was sold once again, along with Selfridge's other provincial stores, to the John Lewis Partnership, with whom they remain to this day. In 1961, the Partnership bought the neighbouring shop, the Bon Marché, on the corner of Basnett Street and Church Street, and amalgamated it with Lee's.

In May 2002, after 149 years of trading under the name of George Henry Lee, the business underwent a name change to John Lewis Liverpool.[18]

In May 2008, Lee's moved from its original building to new purpose-built premises in the Liverpool One retail area, near the Albert Dock.

When Emily Tinne was shopping at Lee's in the 1920s, she appears to have bought mainly coats and hats, with the exception of a couple of camisoles and some items of children's wear. The coats are, like those from Cripps', of excellent quality and would have been quite expensive in black wool facecloth trimmed with chinchilla fur (Cat. no. 53), of nutria fur (Cat. no. 59) and of black silk velvet trimmed with white angora rabbit fur (Cat. no. 66). But Emily also bought a less-expensive evening coat of black rayon grosgrain trimmed with silk fringing (not illustrated, see Appendix, Inventory, 1967.187.47), and it would appear that her mother-in-law, Deborah E. Tinne (1856-1923) had also shopped at Lee's, in earlier years, judging by the two black silk shoulder capes which survive in the Collection and which probably belonged to her (not illustrated, see Appendix, Inventory, 1967.187.5 and WAG 2001.45.1).

The Bon Marché, another shop favoured by Emily Tinne, was founded by the Welshman David Lewis in 1879 when he took over the former Peck's Drapery store. He had already, in 1856, set up Lewis's department store at 44 Ranelagh Street, Liverpool, specialising in the making and retailing of men's and boys' suits. Lewis relied upon two things in the development of this, his first business; his own expertise in the field of tailoring, gained during his apprenticeship in the 1840s with the tailors and outfitters, Benjamin Hyam & Co., of Lord Street, Liverpool, and his knowledge of what the market required – cheap, ready-made clothing. Lewis's store was deliberately aimed at a working-class clientele and prices were kept low by a combination of high-turnover and energetic advertising to appeal to the mass-market.

In 1859, Lewis had set up additional premises in Bold Street, hoping to take some of the lucrative trade from the businesses there, and, in 1864, branched out into women's garments, bonnets and hats. But he could not compete with the leading firms in Bold Street and the shop was not a success. Consequently, his manager, Paul de Jong, encouraged him to look for new premises elsewhere and they discovered Peck's old building in Church Street.

David Lewis's new venture, the Bon Marché, was named after the famous French department store, developed during the 1850s by Aristide Boucicaut in Paris, but with the same retailing values as those of his original store in Ranelagh Street. It was situated next to the more

BON MARCHÉ.

A window at the Bon Marché,
Church Street, about 1900.

Photograph courtesy of the John Lewis Archive.

superior Lee's but was aimed not just at the middle-classes but at all types of customer.

'Inside the Bon Marché, all sorts of goods were on show. From the start men's and boys' clothing was only one feature of the store. Ladies' clothing was advertised, displayed and sold ... Emphasis was laid on the latest French fashions, on "all the novelties from Paris". Perfumery and toilet requisites, infant layettes, umbrellas, patent medicines and boots and shoes, were specialised articles added to the old sales list. By 1880 you could buy American school slates, keyless watches, stationary, books, music and Lewis's "famous two-shilling tea"'.[19]

The Bon Marché grew rapidly. In 1885, the original Peck's building was demolished and a new building erected, complete with a clock tower which became a Liverpool landmark. This, in its turn, was replaced by another building in 1912.

21

Between 1920 and 1924, yet another new store was built above and around the previous one, while the premises remained open to the public. The resulting building, with its clean lines and Art Deco-inspired design was described as 'one of the finest examples of modern architecture that Liverpool possesses'.[20] There were five floors; 'one whole floor devoted to women's attire … Millinery, Costumes, Gowns, Coats and Furs. Everything for boys, girls and babies occupies another whole floor. On the ground floor wide aisles are gay with attractive displays of gloves, umbrellas, handkerchiefs, hosiery etc, while new silks, woollens, cottons, boots, blouses and such like are each presented in delightful departments.'[21]

Like the building it occupied, the Bon Marché promoted itself as Liverpool's most modern, forward-looking department store in the 1920s, and offered its customers a wide range of services. As well as ready-made clothes, there were three different forms of dressmaking available, to suit all pockets. There was the bespoke dressmaking service in the Model Gown Salon, where customers could pay anything between five and fifty guineas for a specially made gown; the Inexpensive Dressmaking Department, where the customer's choice of pattern and fabric from the store's own fabric department could be made up for her, after she had been fitted; and the 'Cut and Fit' Department, where the customer could have her own pattern and fabric cut out and tacked together for her to sew up at home.[22]

Emily seems to have bought mainly hats (including Cat. nos. 145, 151) and fur coats and stoles (Cat. nos. 52, 60, 74, 75) from the Bon Marché, although she also purchased a very stylish French necklace of pearlised plastic and diamanté pastes (Cat. no. 216), and a glamorous evening gown of black satin-backed crepe (Cat. no. 47), fit for a movie star.

Owen Owen Ltd was another of Emily Tinne's favourite places to shop. It was first established as a drapery and haberdashery store at 121 London Road in 1868 by another Welshman, Owen Owen. He set out to capture the Welsh Nonconformist market, a significant part of Liverpool's nineteenth-century population due to the city's proximity to North Wales. Owen went on to invest in further retail development in London, allowing him to raise the funds required for the Liverpool business to expand and develop further.[23] Consequently, in 1925, it moved to a new building in Clayton Square. Moving with the times, and, like the Bon Marché, located in a modern building, Owen Owen Ltd soon had its own Model Gown Department.[24] Emily seems to have bought a wide variety of things from Owen Owen's, including day dresses, coats, fur stoles, hats, underwear and children's items (Cat. nos. 20, 21, 72, 79, 80, 103, 106, 184, 279). She appears to have been particularly fond of machine lace evening dresses with matching lace coatees, as they were known to contemporaries (including Cat. nos. 41, 42), a style which was popular during the later 1920s and well into the 1930s.

Emily appears to have patronised Lewis's department store rather less frequently than the others, judging by surviving items in the collection, possibly because they catered for a more working-class clientele. Nevertheless, there are good examples of shoes and gloves bearing the Lewis's label (including Cat. nos. 139, 188, 195), a moleskin coat (Cat. no. 58) and several fur stoles and cravats (Cat. nos. 76-78).

As already noted, David Lewis had founded the business in Ranelagh Street, Liverpool, in 1856, providing mainly men's and boys' tailoring. Suits were made in great numbers in their own

Hats on display at Owen Owen Ltd, Clayton Square, about 1934.

National Museums Liverpool (Merseyside Maritime Museum, Stewart Bale Archive).

workrooms, behind the premises.[25] The business was successful and expanded in size, until it occupied numbers 34-42, as well as 44 Ranelagh Street. In 1874, Lewis began selling women's and girl's shoes, in 1879 tobacco and cigars, and in the 1880s women's tailored garments, although the men's and boy's garments always remained a strong element in the business.

Lewis's became so well-established that, eventually, branches opened in other British cities; in Manchester in 1880, Sheffield in 1884 and Birmingham in 1885. During the inter-War years, when Emily Tinne was shopping at Lewis's in Liverpool, the store's empire was still growing, with new branches opening in Glasgow in 1929, Leeds in 1932 and Hanley, Stoke-on-Trent, in 1934. Liverpool's Ranelagh Street store finally closed in May 2010 to make way for redevelopment in the area.

Besides the department stores, Emily bought clothes from other well-established Liverpool shops. A number of her hats came from two of Liverpool's high-quality milliners, De Moysey in Ranelagh Street (including Cat. no. 173) and Madame Val Smith in Church Street (including Cat. no. 143).

The firm of De Moysey was founded in 1893 by Madame Emma de Moysey at 11 Parker Street, Liverpool. By 1899, she had acquired number 15 Parker Street as well, and also had

Lewis's and Central Station,
Ranelagh Street, about 1930.

workrooms at 7 and 8 Pembroke Chambers. By 1915 she had moved her premises to the more prestigious Ranelagh Street, where she remained at numbers 37 and 39 until 1941 when she seems finally to have gone out of business.

Madame Val Smith first appears in Liverpool's street directories in 1893 at 21 and 23 Church Street. By 1908 the business appears to have branched out from millinery, describing itself in the directory as a *'wholesale and retail house for millinery, straw hats, felt hats, bonnets, shapes, ribbons and ribbon velvets, flowers, feathers, veilings, gloves, piece silks and velvets and every article required in millinery; also corsets, blouses, skirts, hosiery and ladies' outfitters, furs and fur trimmings of every description'*. By 1941 the firm had moved to 25-27 Basnett Street, where they remained until the early 1970s, before finally finishing trading in Bold Street.

Emily purchased some of her shoes from what was considered Liverpool's smartest shoemaker, J. Collinson & Co. Ltd in Bold Street (Cat. nos. 128, 134) but also from the slightly more down-market W. H. Watts & Co., at Compton House in Church Street (Cat. no. 125), and from Lewis's (Cat. no. 139). Like Lewis's, Watts & Co. were suppliers to the mass-market, importing shoes in great numbers from Europe and America, but Collinson's was much more exclusive.

William Collinson, boot and shoemaker, first moved into 20 Bold Street in 1831, from his original premises in Lord Street, where he had traded for some years previously.[26] By 1839, the

24

Madame Val Smith, Church Street, about 1927.

local street directories list his two sons, James and William, as also being involved in the business, James at 10 Ranelagh Street and William at 36 Bold Street. By 1849, James had taken over both premises and William had re-located to 124 Bold Street. In 1853, Jane Collinson, James' wife, took over the running of his side of the business, following his early death aged only 40, and she appears to have expanded the business to another shop at 17 Elliot Street. It was still relatively rare to find a woman in business on her own account at this time and were usually widows. The 1859 street directory carries an advertisement for the firm with their claim to have '*the largest assortment in the Kingdom of Ladies', Gentlemen's and Children's Ready Made Boots and Shoes, of the very best quality. Wholesale Department and Manufactory, 24, Kings Street, Chester. Merchants and Captains Supplied on the Best of Terms, and on Short Notice*'. Collinson's continued in business in Bold Street until 1972, when they finally closed.

25

Bestway *Outsize Summer Fashions*
with paper pattern for
afternoon dress, about 1929-31.
Accession no. WAG 2003.11.18

Opposite top: Copy of *Weldon's
Smart Fashions for Outsizes*,
including two paper patterns for
dresses, about 1930.
Accession no. 2003.11.19

Opposite bottom: Copy of *Weldon's
Smart Fashions for Wider Hips*,
including three paper patterns
for dresses, about 1932-34.
Accession no. WAG 2003.11.22

THE TINNE COLLECTION OF CLOTHING

The Tinne Collection has come into the possession of the National Museums Liverpool over a long period, and in three separate groups. When Emily Tinne died in 1966, she was living at *Clayton Lodge* with her youngest daughter Alexine, all her other children having long since moved out, some of them to marry and raise families of their own. Philip Tinne had died in 1954. Alexine, unmarried and working as a teacher at a local girls' grammar school, was unwilling to continue occupying such a large house alone, especially when the maintenance costs were becoming onerous. Consequently, she decided to move to a smaller property nearby and had then to undertake the daunting task of disposing of her mother's huge collection of clothes and other effects. In 1966-67 she offered much of this material to the Liverpool Museum. Some 500 or more items were accepted, including day dresses, evening dresses, outdoor garments, underwear, swimwear, shoes, hats, gloves, stockings, jewellery, babywear, children's and servants' clothes, as well as lengths of unworked fabric left over from garments and even some soft household furnishings such as lace curtains and bed coverlets.

In 2001, Alexine Tinne donated a further 162 items, including fur coats and fur-trimmed coats (outdoor garments having been largely and mysteriously missing from the Collection until then), fur stoles, blouses, underwear, children's clothes, gloves and hats. Much of this material had been kept by Elspeth Tinne at her home in Edinburgh and had only come back into Alexine's possession following Elspeth's death in 2000.

Finally, in 2003, Alexine donated another 33 items, including evening dresses, children's clothes, shoes, and, most interesting of all, a collection of 1920s and 1930s fashion magazines and paper dress pattern supplements by makers like Weldon's. Some of these go under such startlingly frank titles as *Smart Fashions for Wider Hips* and *Outsize Underwear*, reflecting the fact that they were bought by Emily at a point in her life when her figure had obviously 'filled out' following the birth of her children.

At over 700 items from the same family, the Tinne Collection is of outstanding size and importance. However, it does not reflect the true nature of Emily's buying, one might almost say systematic collecting, of clothes. There were many more garments which the Museum was unable to accept, mainly because of their poor condition, both in 1967 and subsequently.

It is clear, from what has already been outlined of the family's financial situation, that Emily Tinne's extensive wardrobe was only made possible due to the fact that her husband was a man of substantial private means, over and above what he might have earned as a family doctor.

Copy of *Harrison's Dressmaker*, including a paper pattern for a blouse, October 1916.
Accession no. WAG 2003.11.25

Copy of *Weldon's Matrons*, including paper patterns for two dresses and a coat, 1936.
Accession no. WAG 2003.11.23

Emily's clothes were never ostentatious in style, and indeed were often typical of many of the mainstream fashions of the inter-War period. But due to its sheer volume, her wardrobe is not truly representative of what most middle-class women of the time possessed. Certainly it is doubtful that the wife of an ordinary general practitioner, with no other form of income than his standard fees, might have been able to afford so many clothes.[27]

If one considers the Collection as a whole, certain features are immediately apparent. The first of these concerns the period that it covers. The earliest garments date from just after Emily's marriage in 1910, but strangely there are scarcely any examples (with the exception of some items of underwear and some accessories) which pre-date that point. Why this should be the case is not clear. Alexine Tinne believed that, due to her frugal Scottish Presbyterian background, her mother owned relatively few clothes before her marriage. As a missionary in India, Emily's father, William McCulloch, was a man of modest means and his children had a fairly spartan up-bringing. There was little money available for buying what he viewed as unnecessary luxuries.

Similarly, there is a distinct lack of clothing in the Collection dating from the period after 1939, although this, of course, is more easily explained by the outbreak of the Second World War in that year. One assumes that, from that point onwards, Emily literally had to 'make-do-and-mend' with clothes of the pre-War years, and that clothes rationing and coupons largely put an end to her more excessive shopping.

Looking at each area of the Collection in turn, as laid out in the Catalogue, provides useful insights into the clothing of the middle-class woman in the inter-War years, even though Emily was by no means typical in terms of the sheer volume of things that she owned. Much of her daywear is what one would expect a woman of her age and social position to own in the 1920s and 1930s. She favoured clothes in subdued colours, with muted tones of blue, grey, brown, green and red occurring most frequently, and subtly coloured floral prints. Most of the main developments in dress styles can be seen, from the late Edwardian (Cat. nos. 2-5) through the looser, drop-waisted styles of the 1920s into the sharper, more tailored designs of the early mid-1930s (Cat. nos. 22, 23). Surprisingly, there are no examples of that staple of the middle-class woman's wardrobe, the tailored two-piece suit in plain wool or tweed. Most better-off women possessed such a suit, which could be dressed up for town by the addition of a fur stole, or down for the country by the addition of stout shoes when necessary. Emily Tinne certainly owned many fur stoles but we do not know if they were ever worn with some long-disappeared suit.

One particularly interesting survival among the daywear is the striped silk taffeta bodice with Bertha collar of needlerun net (Cat. no.1) which appears to have been made for maternity wear. It has no bust darts and the voluminous front sections have been designed to expand with the wearer. There are two other examples of maternity wear in the Collection, a black shantung silk dress with over-tunic to disguise the stomach (Appendix, Inventory, Day Clothes, 1967.187.19) and a maternity corset with adjustable side-lacing of about 1920 (Cat. no. 114). Such items are still relatively rare in costume collections generally.

While much of Emily Tinne's daywear appears quite ordinary, elements of higher fashion do feature in certain garments. One good example is the black and red wool afternoon dress of about 1925 (Cat. no. 12) with its plastic buckle featuring two coiled lizards, the design of which is very much influenced by the Art Deco movement. Equally, one can detect a touch of the exotic in the black silk tunic top with silk and gold thread embroidery in the Chinese style (Cat. no. 14), almost certainly imported from China around 1923-25.

The most noticeable thing about Emily Tinne's evening wear is that it is predominantly black, with only the occasional flash of colour. Her daughter Alexine believed that her mother, having once been obliged to put on mourning for some member of the family, found black very convenient thereafter and so continued with it. Certainly, many women today find black both practical and flattering to the figure, so there may be some truth in this theory.

It is not entirely clear exactly when and where the evening garments were worn. The survival of numerous dinner gowns or similar evening dresses indicates that the Tinnes must have dressed for dinner, at least some of the time. But some of the later garments (Cat. nos. 45-47) are too grand for dinner at home and must surely have been worn on some other, more formal, occasion, such as at a party or official function. From family letters, we know that Emily and her husband did go out in the evening, often to the theatre or to local charitable events, when Philip was not busy with an evening surgery for his patients.

Most of Emily's evening clothes were made either by her dressmaker, Mrs Taylor, using patterns from publications such as Weldon's *Semi-Evening Styles for Outsizes*, also in the Collection, or were bought ready-made from department stores such as Owen Owen's (Cat. nos. 41, 42). But several of them were from further afield. The black silk evening dress of about 1910 (Cat. no. 25) by Henry Darling & Co. of Edinburgh may have been ordered as part of her trousseau, on a trip back to Scotland before her marriage. Her wedding dress is by the same maker, although it does not form part of the Collection.[28] More up-market again is the beautifully beaded dress of about 1925 by the Parisian maker Gerlaur (Cat. no. 29). One wonders exactly where this was purchased but we are unlikely ever to know.

Besides the many beaded dresses that she possessed, Emily appears to have been extremely fond of velvets, either plain or devoré, and of the ever-popular machine-made lace evening dress with matching coatee (Cat. nos. 41, 42), available in either a matt or shiny finish. High fashion appears once again, with its Art Deco influence, in a number of dresses with geometric designs and angular patterns (for example, Cat. no. 31), although these tend to be the exception rather than the rule.

Most of Emily Tinne's outdoor garments are either made of or are trimmed with fur of some description, although Alexine did not remember ever having seen her mother wear any of them. Most of the common types of fur used during the 1920s and 1930s are represented, ranging upwards in size from moles to antelopes, and including rabbit, squirrel, sable, mink, fox, beaver, seal, nutria (the fur of the large rodent, the coypu) and Persian lamb. They could vary considerably in price. For example, in 1927, Lewis's in Liverpool were advertising their *'Scotch Moleskin coat, bluey-grey skins of finest quality – exquisitely soft – youthful and straight, with the new "diamond" worked panels back and front'* for £14.10.0.[29] Yet in the same year, The Bon Marché was charging 23 guineas each for one of their diamond moleskin coats.[30] Emily owned three such coats

Copy of *Weldon's Outsize Fashions*, including paper patterns for a dress and a coat, about 1932-34.
Accession no. WAG 2003.11.21

Advertising pamphlet published to celebrate the 75th birthday of George Henry Lee & Co Ltd, 1928. *National Museums Liverpool.*

Copy of *Weldon's Outsize Coats and Frocks*, including paper patterns for two dresses and a coat, 1936.
Accession no.WAG 2003.11.25

Opposite: Copy of *Butterick Fashion News*, November 1935.
Accession no.WAG 2003.11.27

Opposite: Copy of *Weldon's Semi-Evening Styles for Outsizes*, including two paper patterns for dresses, about 1935.
Accession no.WAG 2003.11.29

Opposite: Copy of *Weldon's Outsize Underwear*, including paper patterns for two nightdresses and a petticoat, about 1935.
Accession no.WAG 2003.11.28

(including Cat. no. 58). Plain wool or wool velour coats trimmed with fur were less expensive. In 1927, once again, Lewis's advertised their *'women's fur-trimmed and plain tweed and velour coats'* at 59/6 (or £2.19.6) each.[31] Emily had several examples (including Cat. nos. 49, 51, 53 and 56).

Emily also had a sizable number of fur stoles in her wardrobe, which, in the early 1930s, were often worn with a smart silk day dress when not teamed with a tweed suit, so it is possible that she did actually wear at least some of them. But evidently not the double silver fox fur stole for which she paid 8 guineas (Cat. no. 81) since it still bears its original price tag.

Emily's evening capes and mantles, like many of her evening dresses, reveal her taste for the glamorous, and indeed some of them would not have looked out of place on a Hollywood starlet (for example, Cat. nos. 66, 67). Again, one wonders exactly where she might have worn such dramatic clothes.

Included among the outdoor garments are three short jackets (Cat. nos. 68, 69, 70) which would have been worn largely indoors. They were known to contemporaries as 'bridge coats' and were worn over evening dress while playing after-dinner cards or games. They were popular in the late 1920s and early 1930s. In 1930, Liverpool store T.J. Hughes, which by then had taken over Owen Owen's original premises in London Road, was advertising *'Bridge coats – smart velveteen coats for day or evening wear – 6/11'* while in the same year Henderson's in Church Street was advertising *'A charming and very exclusive collection of Bridge coats, in Chenille, Georgette and Black Chiffon Velvet, some with pure white Foxaline collar and cuffs, others heavily fringed. Silk lined and finished, diamanté clasps, from 59/6'.*[32]

In contrast to some of her more glamorous evening and outdoor clothes, Emily Tinne's blouses and underwear are absolutely typical of their time and include no great surprises, although there are a number of very interesting and now relatively rare early brassières in the Collection (Cat. nos. 110-112). Her swimwear, on the other hand, includes a wonderful early survival, a two-piece wool serge bathing costume with matching cap and espadrilles (Cat. nos. 119-121), which were purchased especially to be worn on her honeymoon in Ireland in 1910.

The bathing costume was made by the firm of L.Y. & J. Nathan of 4 Hardman Street, Liverpool. Lewin Yates and Jane Nathan appear in the Liverpool street directories as *'Shirtmakers, Hosiers and Clerical Outfitters'* from at least the 1860s until the early 1940s, but they also, quite oddly, appear to have sold swimwear too.

Rather disappointingly, Emily's shoes, or at least those that have survived in the Collection, are, on the whole, rather workaday in style. They are all of excellent quality but include no glamorous evening shoes of gold and silver kid leather or brocade, as one might expect, to match her evening dresses. Alexine Tinne recalled that her mother was not especially interested in 'dressy' shoes.

Her huge collection of hats, however, is a different matter. Emily was evidently a great buyer of hats, especially if she could acquire them at a reduced sale price, and those in the Collection are only a proportion of what she once owned since some of them were not accepted by the Museum due to their poor condition. One of the earliest and rarest is the sealskin motoring bonnet with silk chiffon veil (Cat. no. 142). This may well have been worn by Emily when she travelled in what has been claimed as the first ever car in Liverpool, a Daimler Reimenwagen

built by Mercedes-Benz in Stuttgart and imported by her husband's uncle, Theodore Frederick Tinne (1840-1913) in 1896.[33] Upon Theodore's death in 1913, the car was apparently driven by Emily's father-in-law, John Ernest Tinne, before it was eventually abandoned in the old coach-house that once belonged to *Briarley,* some time before the outbreak of the First World War. Since this was the Tinne family's only car at that point it must surely have been the same one in which Emily wore the bonnet. During the First World War, the Daimler was stripped of some of its metal parts, to be melted down for the war-effort, but in 1967 it was rescued and sold back to the Mercedes-Benz Museum in Stuttgart, where it remains today.[34]

Emily's hats reflect the changing styles seen over the period from about 1910 down to the mid-late 1930s. They include numerous examples in glossy black silk and velour, often decorated with delicate egret feathers, hats in natural and coloured straws, and many stylish cloche hats of the late 1920s and early 1930s.[35] Many of these she bought from the well-known city-centre stores, including Cripps in Bold Street (Cat. nos. 164, 165, 168, 169-172), the Bon Marché (Cat. no. 145, 151) and George Henry Lee's (Cat. no. 147) in Church Street and Basnett Street, and Owen Owen Ltd (Cat. no. 184) in Clayton Square, but at least one hat (Cat. no. 154) came from much nearer home, from K. & A. Lennon, Milliners and Costumiers, at 349 Aigburth Road. Owned by (the sisters?) Kate and Anastatia Lennon, this appears to have been a relatively small, local business, literally up the road from *Clayton Lodge*. In addition, there are two hats (Cat. nos. 174 & 175) which were evidently worn by one of the Tinne girls as a teenager.

Emily Tinne's accessories are many and varied, and they include numerous fine examples of gloves, stockings, jabots, hair ornaments, hatpins and costume jewellery. But one type of accessory, the handbag, is noticeable by its absence. While clearing out Clayton Lodge in 1966-67, Alexine Tinne sold several of her mother's beaded evening bags to neighbours and to a local second-hand shop. Other bags were passed on to younger family members, including one of Emily's granddaughters, who still own them today.

The numerous babies' and children's clothes in the Collection are all typical of those worn by middle-class children in the period from about 1910 down to the 1930s. They include the Tinne family christening gown (Cat. no. 240), worn by all of Emily's children between 1911, when Elspeth was born, and 1929 when her last child, Pip, was born. It is beautifully made, of white cotton lawn, embroidered in white with swags and bows and cutwork butterflies. But much more unusual and a rare survival is the pair of white glazed earthenware sock-dryers (Cat. no 282), made by Wedgwood sometime in the period between 1907 and 1924. Damp socks were drawn on over them and left to dry in shape.

There are few examples of branded children's garments, with one or two exceptions. These include the items of Eton school uniform worn by Ernest Tinne and made by John Walls Ltd, of 13 & 14 High Street, Eton (Appendix, Inventory, 1967.187.170) and the young girl's sailor-style tunic-top, probably worn by Elspeth Tinne and made by Hope Brothers Ltd (Cat. no. 263). Hope Brothers were a large-scale supplier of children's school uniforms and other garments, with branches in London and throughout the country. Their Liverpool premises were at 99-101 Lord Street, which is where Emily probably purchased this tunic-top.

Emily's motivation for buying clothes in such volume is unclear. Set free, upon her marriage, from the constraints of her Presbyterian up-bringing, and with access to money for the first time in her life, she appears to have embarked upon shopping with a passion. Certainly, both Alexine Tinne and her sister Helen recalled their mother going shopping almost every afternoon, much as one pursues a hobby. This may suggest that she was an early example of that modern phenomenon, the 'shopaholic', the compulsive buyer who purchases items to fulfil an emotional need or to combat boredom. Emily was an intelligent woman, but contemporary social convention prevented married women from working, so shopping may have filled the void for her. She had domestic staff to help care for her children and, consequently, time on her hands. That Emily may have been driven by a compulsion to buy is a view that Alexine Tinne did not dismiss, especially given her mother's habit of sometimes purchasing multiple examples of the same garment in different colourways, often leaving them unworn. Many items in the collection still retain their original price labels and some were even in the original tissue paper and boxes in which they were delivered to *Clayton Lodge*, complete with dates, which is extremely useful from a museum point of view. Emily seems to have been especially attracted to sale bargains, with many labelled items having been marked down from their original prices. For example, in about 1925 she purchased a blue ribbed silk coat from Owen Owen's (1967.187.32, not illustrated), for £12, reduced from the

Copy of *Weldon's Bazaar of Children's Fashions*, including paper patterns for a child's dress and dolls' clothes, September 1914. *Accession no. WAG 2003.11.23*

Copy of *Weldon's Smart Outsizes*, including paper patterns for two dresses and a coat, 1936. *Accession no. WAG 2003.11.30*

Copy of *Weldon's Matrons' Winter Styles*, including paper patterns for two dresses and a coat, 1936. *Accession no. WAG 2003.11.24*

original £18, the equivalent of some £534 in modern terms.[36] Day dresses were often cheaper. A printed rayon crepe dress from Owen Owen's in about 1930-32 (Cat. no. 21) cost 20 shillings, the equivalent of about £53 today. But evening wear and furs could be much more expensive. One of her favourite machine lace ensembles, such as that from Owen Owen's of about 1934-36 (Cat. no. 42) cost 94/6, or £4.10s.6d.; about £245 in modern terms. The two moleskin stoles she purchased from the Bon Marché in 1926, at 17 guineas for the two (Cat. nos. 74 & 75) would cost in the region of £808 today.

It is possible that there may have been an element of philanthropy to Emily's buying. Alexine believed that her mother bought many of her clothes simply as a way of providing some of Liverpool's poorly paid shop assistants with the much-needed commission during the Depression years. Certainly this may be true of the numerous expensive fur coats that Emily possessed, especially given the fact that she does not appear to have worn them, at least not on a regular basis.

The volume of clothes purchased by Emily did not go unnoticed by Philip Tinne, according to Alexine, and even caused a certain amount of tension between her parents on occasion. There were so many clothes that a normal bedroom wardrobe would not have accommodated them. Ironically, Mrs Tinne's actual wardrobe, a wedding gift to her and Philip in 1910 from her friend Mrs Waring, by the furniture makers Waring and Gillow, must soon have been full. Alexine remembered that many of her mother's clothes were then stored in a bathroom located off her parent's bedroom, which eventually became a storeroom and so could not be used for its original purpose. When this was full, the disused servants' quarters over the stables were used, probably from the early 1940s onwards, and at least part of the Collection was housed there up until 1967 when it was donated to the Museum. But the bulk of Emily's clothes were stored in numerous tea-chests in the cellar of *Clayton Lodge,* where, in about 1940, while England feared an imminent German invasion, she began to stack them up to form a solid wall of boxes. They were used to block off access to the cellar's many rooms, where Emily had stored other valuables, including china, wine and jewellery. And there they stayed until Alexine began to clear the house in 1966.

Whatever Emily's motivations for buying so many garments really were, one should not discount the idea that she simply enjoyed shopping and was good at it. Ultimately, we can only be thankful that her buying sprees were so extensive, resulting in such a wonderfully complete and varied wardrobe of clothes.

ENDNOTES

Alexandrina Petronella Francina Tinne (1835-69), the half-sister of Philip Tinne's grandfather, was a noted traveller and an early explorer of the Nile and the Sudan. She was killed in 1869 during an encounter with Tuareg tribesmen in the Sahara. See 'Alexandrine (sic) Tinne, African Explorer', in *Six Life Studies of Famous Women*, Matilda Betham-Edwards, 1880, pp.41-86, and *Travels of Alexine: Alexine Tinne, 1835-1869*, Penelope Gladstone, London, 1970. For the most recent account of her travels, see *The Fateful Journey, The Expedition of Alexine Tinne and Theodor von Heuglin in Sudan (1863-1864)*, Robert Joost Willink, Amsterdam University Press, 2011.

Two of Alexandrina's garments, a dress and petticoat, from when she was a child, survive in the Collection (See Appendix, Inventory, Babies' and Children's Clothes, WAG 2001.45.68 & 69). She is depicted wearing the dress in an 1839 portrait of her aged about three or four, by the Belgian artist, Jan Baptist van der Hulst (1790-1862), Court painter at The Hague between 1830 and 1849. I am grateful to my colleague Xanthe Brooke, Curator of Continental European Fine Art at the Walker Gallery, for this information. The portrait remains in the possession of the Tinne family.

2. Tinne family photographs of this wedding still exist, showing Emily dressed as a bridesmaid. The groom, John A. Tinne, became M.P. for Wavertree, Liverpool, in 1924.

3. *History of British Guiana*, J. Rodway, 1893. Cited at www.casbah.ac.uk, a description of the Casbah Collection (Caribbean Studies, Black and African History), Institute of Commonwealth Studies, London.

4. The British Parliament passed the Slavery Abolition Act on 24 August 1833 but it did not become law until 1 August 1834, when all slaves in the British colonies were freed.

5. See *Sandbach, Tinne & Co, West India Merchants of Liverpool*, Eunice Shanahan at www.scholars.nus.edu.sg/victorian/history/letters/sandfin.html The Sandbach Tinne Papers form part of the Bryson Collection and are held in the Merseyside Maritime Museum's Maritime Archives Department. They deal with such topics as the Demerara plantations and their management, 1795-1870. An account of a number of the firm's ships can be found in *The 'Sandbach' of Liverpool*, by E.W. Argyle in *Sea Breezes*, Vol. 9, 1950, pp.141-143. To convert contemporary money to modern values see Lawrence H. Officer and Samuel H. Williamson, 'Purchasing Power of British Pounds from 1245 to Present', MeasuringWorth, 2011.

6. The inventory is still in the possession of the Tinne family.

7. See *Purchasing Power of British Pounds from 1245 to Present*, op. cit.

8. *The Story of the Tinne Family*, John Ernest Tinne, unpublished, not dated, p.39.

9. Obituary of Philip Frederic Tinne, *Liverpool Daily Post*, 30 January, 1954.

10. 'But Dr Tinne will be most remembered for his work for the poor in Garston, where he was the friend of many families', Obituary, *Liverpool Echo*, 29 January, 1954.

11. Obituary of Philip Frederic Tinne, *Liverpool Daily Post*, 30 January, 1954.

12. Recalled by Mrs Margaret Bolton of Aigburth, July 2004. Between 1933 and 1946, Mrs Bolton also worked for Sandbach, Tinne & Co. as a typist at their main offices in Cook Street, Liverpool. She started on 15 shillings per week, typing out the details of the firm's sugar imports and exports, and by the time she left in 1946 was earning 25 shillings per week. Mrs Bolton remembers them fondly as a good firm to work for, with strong philanthropic leanings. For example, they always took on boys from the Bluecoat Orphanage and from the Liverpool Seaman's Orphanage as office boys.

13. See *Purchasing Power of British Pounds from 1245 to Present*, op. cit.

14. I am grateful to Susan Howe, a former neighbour of the Tinne family, for this information.

15. Fraser's *Guide to Liverpool*, Liverpool, 1861, pp.255-56.

16. Idem.

17. *Liverpool Fashion, Its Makers and Wearers. The Dressmaking Trade in Liverpool, 1830-1940*, Anthea Jarvis, Liverpool, 1981, p.21.

18. *The Liverpool Echo*, 13 May, 2002.

19. *Friends of the People; The Centenary History of Lewis's*, Asa Briggs, London, 1956, p.38.

20. *The Story of Liverpool*, London Assurance, 1925, p.22.

21. *Cox's Liverpool Annual and Year Book*, 1924, p.305.

22. *Liverpool Fashion*, op.cit., pp.41-42.

23. *The Department Store, A Social History*, Bill Lancaster, London and New York, 1995, p.40.

24. *Liverpool Fashion*, op.cit., p.41.

25. 'Lewis & Company's Establishment is exclusively devoted to supplying Boys' Clothing, Boys' Boots, Boys' Caps, Boys' Shirts and Stockings and every requisite from top to toe, exclusively for Boys from 6 years old to 20. It is the only Establishment of the kind in the world. Fifty thousand Boys are annually supplied with clothing at this novel Establishment, and the Proprietors are unceasing in their efforts to give the utmost unqualified satisfaction.' See *Friends of the People*, op.cit., p.33.

26. *The Liverpool Mercury*, 16 September, 1831.

27. For a comparison of how many garments the more typical middle-class woman bought during this period, and how much she paid for them, see Katina Bill, *Clothing Expenditure by a Woman in the Early 1920s*, in *Costume*, No.27, 1993, pp.57-60. This details some of the clothes worn between 1920 and 1923 by Mrs Mary Pennyman, of Ormesby Hall, Middlesbrough, who is described as '*a member of an established county family*'.

28. Henry Darling & Co., Silk Mercers, were in business from 1893-1970. They started off at 124 Princes Street, Edinburgh, and by 1901 had acquired 123 and 124a Princes Street. In 1945 they changed from being Silk Mercers to 'Ladies' Outfitters', and by 1966 had become known as 'Darlings of Edinburgh'.

I am grateful to Susan Varga, Library Officer at the City of Edinburgh Archives, and to Fiona Anderson, Curator of Costume at the National Museum of Scotland, for this information.

Emily Tinne's wedding dress is now in the Grosvenor Museum, Chester, where it was donated in 1986 by her daughter, Mrs Helen Orry. It is of cream silk with a wrap-over neckline and wrap-over skirt with a short train. After the wedding it was altered, with the net bodice in-fill and high collar being removed, to allow it to be worn as a ball gown. Unfortunately, it is now in a rather poor state, the tin-weighted silk from which it is made having split badly along the grain.

I am grateful to Hannah Crowdy, former Keeper of Local and Social History at the Grosvenor, for information about this dress and for allowing me to examine it.

Helen Tinne wore her mother's wedding dress for her own wedding to Gordon Orry at St Anne's Church, Aigburth, Liverpool, on 10 April 1948. St Anne's was built by Helen's grandfather, John Abraham Tinne, together with a number of his business associates, in 1837. He regarded its building as an act of thanks for having survived the shipwreck of the S.S. *Rothesay Castle*, which sank off Beaumaris, Anglesey, on 17 August 1831.

29. Advertisement for Lewis's, *The Liverpool Echo*, 5 October, 1927.

30. Advertisement for the Bon Marché, *The Liverpool Echo*, 13 October, 1927.

31. Advertisement for Lewis's, *The Liverpool Echo*, 14 September, 1927.

32. Advertisements for T.J. Hughes', and for Henderson's, both in *The Liverpool Echo*, 17 and 25 September, 1930.

33. Recorded in John Ernest Tinne's unpublished work, *The Story of the Tinne Family*, p.38.

34. The car was sold for £5,000. It is a four seater with a two cylinder in-line 3hp engine. I am grateful to Christoph Knecht and Jens Schmitt of the DaimlerChrysler Museum, Stuttgart, for confirming these details.

35. Emily owned a number of straw hats (including Cat. no.156) similar to those described by T.J. Rendell, a milliner at Liberty's, London, in the mid-late 1920s;

'One of our main jobs in the summer was making raffia embroidered hats ... Originally our stockroom had purchased a few from Italy and it was decided that our workroom could do something like it. So we obtained ordinary straw hoods, probably Oriental and Italian, with a deep crown and a wide brim, and plenty of dyed raffia in many colours and got to work. The design was more or less made up as we went along, starting with big daisy-like flowers in front and filling in with roses and smaller flowers and leaf shapes over the rest of the crown.' She also describes how cloche hats were made. See T.J. Rendell, *Millinery Techniques in the 1920s*, in *Costume*, No.12, 1978, pp.86-94.

36. All prices are approximate. See *Purchasing Power of British Pounds from 1245 to Present*, op. cit.

DAY CLOTHES

1. Maternity or nursing bodice (?), silk taffeta, about 1911-15

Bodice of lilac, black and white striped silk taffeta, cut very wide across the bodice, without bust darts. Fastens down the centre front with hooks and eyes. Wide, pagoda sleeves edged with cotton lace braid, deep Bertha collar and engageantes of needlerun net.

Probably worn by Emily Tinne during her early pregnancies.

Other maternity clothes survive in the collection. See Catalogue, no. 114, and Appendix, Day Clothes, accession no. 1967.187.19

Accession no. WAG 2001.45.3

2. Day dress, cotton voile, about 1910

Summer day dress, pale blue, green and white striped cotton voile. Softly pleated bodice, lined with white cotton, high-necked insert and cuffs of spotted cotton net and machine-made lace. Sleeves each have six tucks. Voile rosette at centre back of bodice.

Accession no. 1967.187.10

3. Day dress, cotton lawn, about 1910-12

Summer day dress of white cotton lawn, the bodice, three-quarter length sleeves and skirt all decorated with machine-made whitework embroidery and inserted bands of machine-made lace. Ruffle of torchon bobbin lace around the neckline.

Accession no. 1967.187.12

4. Day dress, wool, about 1912-14

Day dress of blue wool with wide, elbow-length sleeves. Skirt fastens down left-hand side with press-studs, disguised by six large buttons covered with black velvet and cream silk braid. Bodice, neckline and outer edge of sleeves all decorated with applied bands of black silk velvet. Wool-covered buttons and buttonholes of cream silk rick rack braid. Bodice lined with cream-coloured nun's veiling.

This dress has been altered in the bodice, and is possibly made from an earlier skirt and bodice with new trimmings applied later. It may have been adapted for wear as a maternity or nursing dress.

Accession no. 1967.187.7

5. Day dress, wool, about 1912

Day dress of grey wool, the bodice lined with cream silk satin, the skirt front lined with pale grey silk. Bodice and cuffs on the three quarter-length sleeves both embroidered with geometric and floral patterns in grey silk. V-shaped neckline decorated with applied grey silk braid. Undersleeves and detachable, high-necked bodice insert both of pale grey embroidered net.

Accession no. 1967.187.8

6. Day dress, cotton velvet, about 1914-16

Day dress of blue cotton velvet, the V-shaped neckline, centre front edge and cuffs all trimmed with brown fox fur. Cuffs cut slightly over the hand and lined with pale blue and pink shot silk. Butterfly motifs of applied metal thread and glass beads on left side of bodice, right back of bodice and skirt. Bodice lined with white cotton.

Inside of skirt stamped *WORRALL'S FAST DYE, Does not rub off, JA.s & Jn. & M.Worrall, Warranted, Fast Finish,* and *WORRALL, DYED FAST COLOR* (sic).

This dress has a matching draw-string bag of blue cotton velvet lined with blue cotton sateen, trimmed with fox fur and decorated with applied metallic thread butterfly motifs.
Accession no. 1967.187.14

7. Day dress, rayon jersey, about 1914-16

Day dress of blue machine-knitted rayon jersey, with wide scooped neckline and elbow-length sleeves. Plain belted waistline. Decorated around neckline, sleeves and down sides of bodice with chain stitch machine-embroidery in pale grey silk. Fully lined with pale blue silk.
Accession no. 1967.187.63

8. Day dress, silk, about 1914-16

Day dress of navy blue and grey silk, with wide scooped neckline and elbow-length sleeves. Bodice and skirt front decorated with contrasting hand-embroidery in navy blue and grey. Navy blue silk sash, with navy blue and white silk tassels, fastening on the right-hand side of the waist. Bodice lined with white cotton muslin.
Accession no. 1967.187.62

9. Day dress, tussah silk, about 1916-18

Summer day dress of natural-coloured tussah silk. Bodice fastens down centre front with four ball-shaped plastic buttons, and with two more buttons at the waistband. Long sleeves with pointed, turned-back cuffs. Bodice front, cuffs, skirt front and sides are all decorated with floral hand-embroidery in natural-coloured silk. Bodice and sleeve tops are also decorated with faggoting. Unlined.
Accession no. 1967.187.18

10. Day dress, rayon silk, about 1922-23

Day dress of blue rayon silk, with wide three-quarter length sleeves. Skirt slightly gathered on the hips and horizontally pleated in the centre front. Self tie belt. Rounded collar and centre front panel of bodice both of pale grey silk crepe. Bodice and skirt front both decorated with deep band of pale grey machine-embroidered silk in stylised floral pattern. Bodice lined with blue cotton net.
Accession no. 1967.187.59

11. Day dress, silk and rayon, about 1924-25

Day dress of brown, white and orange printed silk. V-shaped neckline, the collar and cuffs both double ruffles of machine-made lace. Band at centre front of dress, the dropped waistline, hemline and cuff edgings are all of dark brown ribbed rayon. Slightly longer, tubular under-slip of dark brown silk.

This dress has a matching duster coat of dark brown ribbed rayon trimmed with the same printed silk (not illustrated. See Appendix, Outdoor Clothes and Furs, accession no. 1967.187.20).
Accession no. 1967.187.21

Detail, Cat. no. 11.

12. Afternoon dress, wool crepe, about 1925

Afternoon dress of black wool crepe, the central insert of wool crepe sewn from neckline to hem with small red wool circles. Narrow revers also sewn with red wool circles. Low waistline marked by band of horizontal pin-tucks. Hook and eye fastenings at centre front, hidden by circular plastic buckle in the form of two curling lizards. Long sleeves with deep band of pin-tucks at cuffs. Plain black silk under-slip, attached to central insert.

Accession no. 1967.187.24

Detail, Cat. no. 12.

13. Afternoon dress, silk crepe, about 1925

Afternoon dress of terracotta brown silk crepe, the bodice slashed in the centre front to reveal panel of pale brown silk crepe. Dropped waistline and cuffs both decorated with chain stitch embroidery in terracotta and brown silk and gold metallic thread, now tarnished. Deep panel of terracotta-coloured silk fringing falls over skirt from waistband. Silk crepe corsage attached to left shoulder. Bodice lined with white silk.
Accession no. 1967.187.25

14. Tunic top, silk and silk satin, about 1923-25

Tunic top with scooped neckline, the front and back of black silk, the long sleeves, wrist-ties and bottom edges of tunic of silk satin. Front and lower section of back are both hand-embroidered in tambour stitch with Chinoiserie design in pale blue silk and gold metallic thread, now tarnished. Unlined.
Labelled *L & M, KOM: 833, FAC: 5773, 44*
Probably made in China for European export.
Accession no. WAG 2001.45.28

15. Afternoon dress, silk satin and silk damask, about 1925-27

Afternoon dress of aubergine-coloured silk satin and silk damask. Long V-shaped neckline crosses over in centre front. Dropped waistline with aubergine silk belt and draped skirt front, held by oval-shaped silver metal buckle on left-hand side. Under-slip of pale aubergine-coloured silk.

Accession no. 1967.187.22

16. Afternoon dress, silk velvet devoré, about 1927-28

Afternoon dress of dark red silk velvet devoré, worked in a large floral pattern. Central panel, neckties and cuffs all of red silk crepe, the panel and neckties both decorated with narrow, flat, vertical pleats. Dropped waistline, marked at centre front by four square buckles of metal, enamelled red and edged with diamanté pastes. Under-slip of dark red silk crepe.

Accession no. 1967.187.511

17. Day dress, silk chiffon, about 1929-32

Summer day dress of black silk chiffon, printed all over with small floral pattern in pale blue, cream and brown. Square neckline with V-shaped insert of cream silk crepe and long, draped revers. Long sleeves with horizontal tuck at cuff. Silver metal brooch set with yellow plastic bead at bottom of neckline. Bodice and pleated skirt both lined with plain black silk.

Accession no. 1967.187.29

18. Day dress, silk crepe, about 1930-32

Summer day dress, navy blue silk crepe printed with floral pattern in green, pale blue, orange and white. Flared skirt, long sleeves with ruffles above elbow, V-shaped neckline with tie at front and flesh-coloured silk crepe insert, decorated with horizontal pin-tucks. Narrow belt of printed crepe. Unlined.
Accession no. 1967.187.81

19. Day dress, cotton and rayon crepe, about 1930-32

Summer day dress, blue cotton and rayon crepe printed with floral pattern in green, white, pink, pale blue and orange. Square neckline with deep collar and long, V-shaped insert of flesh-coloured silk crepe. Printed cotton and rayon crepe belt with small blue plastic buckle at centre front. Two pleats to either side of skirt front. Long plain sleeves. Unlined.
Labelled *OS, 46*
Accession no. 1967.187.76

20. Day dress, cotton and rayon crepe, about 1930-32

Summer day dress, blue cotton and rayon crepe, printed with stylised flower and leaf design in green, yellow, orange and white. V-shaped neckline with fall collar and oval-shaped insert of flesh-coloured silk crepe, with four plastic buttons. Printed crepe belt with blue plastic buckle to centre front. Inverted pleat to either side of skirt front. Long plain sleeves. Unlined. Labelled *OWEN OWEN LTD, LIVERPOOL, Stock No.Q25, Dept No.51, Style 4041, Size OS, Price 12/6 and OS, 48*
Accession no. 1967.187.78

21. Day dress, rayon crepe, about 1930-32

Summer day dress, royal blue rayon crepe printed with daisies in red, white, pink and green. Fall collar with ties over V-shaped pleated insert of flesh-coloured rayon crepe. Inverted pleats to either side of skirt front. Printed crepe belt. Long sleeves with narrow diagonal band of flesh-coloured crepe. Labelled *OWEN OWEN LTD, LIVERPOOL, Stock No.Q22, Dept No.51, Size OS, Price 20/-*
Accession no. 1967.187.80

22. Day dress, rayon jersey, about 1932-35

Day dress of black knitted rayon jersey with looped-pile textured surface. V-shaped neckline with white rayon satin trim and pleated black jersey frill, the ends backed with white rayon satin. Two large black plastic buttons. Long plain sleeves. Half tie-belt at centre back. Unlined. Labelled *Melso Fabric, British Made* and *F322, No.1603, Lgth. 50, Size 50, British Make*
Accession no. 1967.187.73

23. Day dress, wool crepe, about 1932-35

Day dress of navy blue wool crepe. Tie neckline of navy and ice blue rayon silk. Inverted pleat to centre front of bodice, stitching detail and two oval-shaped blue plastic buttons. Wool crepe belt with two more oval-shaped blue plastic buttons. Two inverted pleats to skirt front, two triangular-shaped patch pockets with stitching detail. Long sleeves with stitching detail to turned-back cuffs. Unlined.

Accession no. 1967.187.69

24. Day dress, rayon crepe, about 1935

Day dress of navy blue rayon crepe printed with stylised wheat-ear design in white. Plain rounded neckline with applied rayon jabot and row of five small covered buttons down centre front. Long plain sleeves and tie belt. Unlined.

Accession no. 1967.187.110

EVENING CLOTHES

25. Evening dress, silk, about 1910

Evening dress of black silk, draped bodice with square-cut neckline, insert of horizontally pleated white silk net, trimmed with metallic silver braid. Short ruched sleeves edged with white silk net and metallic silver braid. Raised waistline of pleated black silk, with 'buckle' of applied silver braid. Applied ruffle to hemline of skirt. Bodice lined with black glazed cotton, skirt unlined. Dress-band woven with *HENRY DARLING & CO., EDINBURGH*
Accession no. 1967.187.13

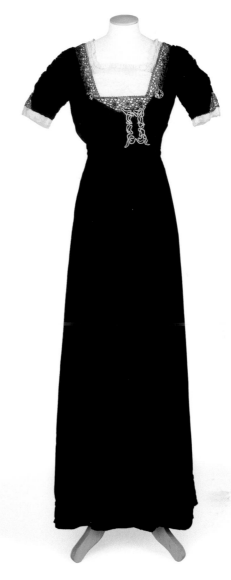

26. Evening dress, machine-made lace, silk chiffon and cotton sateen, about 1921-23

Evening dress of black silk machine-made lace, in a geometric pattern, lined with black cotton sateen. Scooped neckline, the yoke and full-length open sleeves of black silk chiffon. Sleeves fasten at the wrist with narrow silk chiffon band. Low waistline with pleated black silk satin sash, knotted on the left-hand side. Two tiers of lace to the skirt.
Accession no. 1967.187.43

27. Evening dress, silk crepe, about 1924-25

Evening dress of black silk crepe. Square neckline with fall collar and V-shaped insert of black silk crepe. Bodice lined with plain white silk. Front of bodice and skirt and scalloped hemline all decorated with applied silver and bronze-coloured metal beads. Long sleeves gathered into cuff, also decorated with metal beads.
Accession no. 1976.187.56

28. Evening dress, silk and silk crepe, about 1925

Sleeveless evening dress of black silk crepe with V-shaped neckline. Separate, scoop-necked under-slip of black silk with yoke of silk crepe. Bodice completely covered with applied black and grey bugle beads in a large floral pattern, the skirt with scalloped hemline also sewn with vertical bands of glass bugle beads.
Labelled *Made in France*
Accession no. 1967.187.54

29. Evening dress, silk crepe and rayon jersey, about 1925

Evening dress of black silk crepe with wide boat neckline and short sleeves. Separate under-slip of machine-knitted black rayon jersey with scooped neckline. Front and back of bodice and skirt decorated with applied clear and silver glass bugle beads and tiny oval-shaped mirrors, worked in a scrolling pattern. Two V-shaped godets of black silk crepe at sides of the skirt.
Labelled *Gerlaur, 33 FAUBOURG POISSONNIÈRE, Paris*
Accession no. 1967.187.55

Detail, Cat. no. 29.

30. Evening dress, silk crepe and silk, about 1925

Evening dress of black silk crepe with wide scooped neckline. Separate under-slip of plain black silk. Bodice and skirt almost completely covered with applied black plastic sequins and glass bugle beads. Wide, open-seamed sleeves, weighted with tassels of bugle beads. Low waistline, decorated on left-hand side with large rosette of pink and purple silk crepe and silk velvet.
Accession no. 1967.187.53

31. Evening dress, silk and silk chiffon, about 1925-27

Sleeveless evening dress of black silk chiffon woven with a pattern of geometric shapes and stylised roses in silver thread. Square neckline with V-shaped insert of black silk chiffon. Cross-over bodice front with long revers. Large rosette of cerise pink cotton voile on the left-hand side. Lined with plain black silk.
Accession no. 1967.187.52

32. Evening dress, silk and silk crepe, about 1928-30

Sleeveless evening dress of black silk crepe. Separate under-slip of plain black silk. Square neckline with deep, scooped insert of black silk crepe, decorated around the edge with applied loops of black and clear glass beads. Front of bodice, just below waistline, decorated with large appliquéd palm motif in diamanté pastes and glass beads. Silk crepe gathered and draped down left side of dress.

Accession no. WAG 2003.11.3

33. Evening dress, silk and silk crepe, about 1928-30

Evening dress of black silk crepe with rounded neckline. Separate under-slip of plain black silk with V-shaped neckline. Inverted pleats to either side of skirt front. Both bodice and skirt decorated with applied iridescent glass bugle beads in a stylised floral pattern. Long sleeves with silk crepe ties at wrists.

Accession no. WAG 2003.11.2

34. Dinner dress, silk velvet devoré, about 1932-34

Dinner dress of dark blue silk velvet devoré, worked in a floral pattern. Cross-over bodice front edged with machine-made lace and secured on the left side of the waistline by a white metal brooch set with diamanté pastes. Long sleeves with applied ruffles above the cuffs. Separate under-slip of dark blue silk.

Accession no. 1967.187.513

35. Dinner dress and matching coatee, silk crepe and silk velvet, about 1932-34

Sleeveless dinner dress of black silk crepe, the bodice and skirt with a raised silk velvet pile, printed with flowers and a fish-scale pattern in orange, yellow, blue and pale brown V-shaped neckline, with tie at either side, both decorated with applied printed velvet. White metal and diamanté paste brooch at centre front of waistline. Matching long-sleeved coatee, the cuffs decorated with a band of the same printed velvet. Separate under-slip of black silk crepe.

Accession no. 1967.187.85

36. Dinner dress and matching coatee, silk panne velvet devoré, about 1932-34

Sleeveless dinner dress of gunmetal grey silk panne velvet devoré, with draped bodice back and front and panelled, flared skirt. V-shaped neckline, separate under-slip of pale grey silk crepe with scooped neckline and scalloped hem. Matching long-sleeved coatee with long scallop-edge revers, fastening at centre front with two filigree white metal buttons. Applied scallop-edged frill above cuffs and corsage of grey silk crepe and velvet on left shoulder.

Accession no. 1967.187.84

37. Dinner dress and matching coatee, silk velvet, about 1932-34

Sleeveless dinner dress of dark blue and black silk velvet, printed all over with tulips in cream and pale blue. V-shaped neckline, back and front. Cross-over bodice front fastening on left-hand side with white metal clip set with diamanté pastes. Flared, tiered skirt, partly lined with black rayon silk. Flat velvet bow attached to left shoulder. Matching long-sleeved coatee, crossing over at centre front to fasten on left-hand side with gold metal filigree clasp, set with blue stones. Scalloped hemline to coatee.

Accession no. 1967.187.83

38. Dinner dress, silk panne velvet devoré, about 1932-35

Dinner dress of dusty pink silk panne velvet devoré, worked in a stylised floral pattern. V-shaped neckline with insert of machine-embroidered flesh-coloured silk crepe. Long, narrow revers finishing in bow at centre front of waistline. Long sleeves, flared skirt. Unlined.

Accession no. 1967.187.91

39. Dinner dress, machine-made lace and silk crepe, about 1934-36

Dinner dress of bottle-green machine-made lace, with inserted diagonal bands and flared godets of green silk crepe. Square neckline with draped collar of silk crepe, held on left side by white metal brooch set with green glass and diamanté pastes. Similar clasp, also set with green glass and diamanté pastes, at centre front of crepe belt. Bodice and long, slightly flared sleeves all lined with green crepe. Fully lined with plain green silk.
Accession no. 1967.187.98

40. Dinner dress, machine-made lace, silk crepe and rayon satin, about 1934-36

Dinner dress, the bodice and part of the long sleeves of dark brown machine-made lace. V-shaped neckline. Panelled, flared skirt of brown silk crepe. Upper part of sleeves and cuffs also of silk crepe. Brown silk crepe belt with white metal buckle set with diamanté pastes at centre front. Fully lined with brown rayon satin.
Accession no. 1967.187.97

41. Evening dress and matching coatee, machine-made lace and rayon taffeta, about 1934-36

Full-length sleeveless evening dress of black machine-made lace, worked in a large daisy pattern. Flared skirt and V-shaped neckline with diamanté paste clip at centre front. Matching lace coatee with long sleeves and flared cuffs. Separate under-slip of black rayon taffeta.
Labelled *OWEN OWEN LTD, LIVERPOOL, Stock No. X18, Dept No. 11.131, Style 2432, Size 50, Price 63/-*
Accession no. 1967.187.103

42. Evening dress and matching coatee, machine-made lace and silk, about 1934-36

Full-length sleeveless evening dress of black machine-made lace with V-shaped neckline. Flared skirt with scallop-edged lace frill attached down centre front and back. Matching lace coatee with scallop-edged collar and revers, three quarter-length sleeves with turn-back cuffs and silk satin edging. Fastens at centre front with lace belt and oval-shaped gilt glass buckle. Separate under-slip of black silk with deep, scallop-edged border of black cotton net. Labelled *OWEN OWEN LTD, LIVERPOOL, Stock No. N15, Dept No. 24, Colour No. J, Size OS, Price 94/6* on coatee, and *Patriana* on under-slip

Accession no. 1967.187.106

43. Evening dress, rayon crepe and machine-made lace, about 1935-36

Full-length evening dress of deep purple rayon crepe, the bodice with halter neckline, crossing over in the front and decorated with two large buttons covered with diamanté pastes. Bodice front and flared cape-like sleeves all of purple machine-made lace. Bias-cut skirt. Unlined.

Labelled *D.K. No. 3046, STYLE No. 954X, SIZE & COL., 4F, MACHINIST Penny, FINISHER, PRESSER, HOUSE Wain (?)*

Accession no. 1967.187.99

44. Evening dress, silk satin-backed crepe and silk chiffon, about 1935-36

Full-length evening dress of black silk satin-backed crepe, with bolero-effect bodice. V-shaped neckline over black silk chiffon insert, woven with leaf pattern in silver thread and lined with pale pink silk crepe. Centre front decorated with woven leaf motifs in silver thread. Intricately cut sleeves, the tops and cuffs of black crepe, the puffed central sections of silk chiffon woven with leaf motifs in silver thread. Flared, panelled skirt. Unlined.

Accession no. 1967.187.95

45. Evening dress, silk crepe and silk chiffon, about 1935-36

Full-length sleeveless evening dress of heavy black silk crepe. Draped cowl neckline. Decorated around armholes and down sides of dress with vertical rows of applied black plastic sequins. Wide, semi-circular sleeve drapes of black silk chiffon over arm holes. Plain black crepe belt at waistline. Unlined.

Accession no. 1967.187.92

46. Evening dress, silk satin-backed crepe and silk crepe, about 1935-36

Full-length sleeveless evening dress of black silk satin-backed crepe, bias-cut and close fitting. Soft V-shaped neckline at front, deep V-neckline at back. Triangular-shaped shoulder drapes of black crepe, lined with white silk crepe, attached at shoulders. Dress covered with applied glass beads in large circular pattern, in clear glass on bodice and upper skirt, and in black glass on the lower skirt and shoulder drapes. Beaded black silk crepe belt and circular buckle. Unlined.

Labelled *No. 8319, Dkt 4781*

Accession no. 1967.187.93

47. Evening dress, silk satin-backed crepe and silk satin, about 1935-36

Full-length sleeveless evening dress of black silk satin-backed crepe, bias cut and close fitting. High V-shaped neckline at front, deep V-neckline at back. Long wing-shaped shoulder drapes of black satin-backed crepe, lined with pale pink silk satin, attached at shoulders by clasps of black and clear plastic and diamanté pastes. Narrow belt of satin-backed crepe secured with plastic and diamanté paste clasp. Unlined.

Labelled *AN Olive Scott MODEL* and *BON MARCHÉ, LIVERPOOL, LTD*

Accession no. 1967.187.87

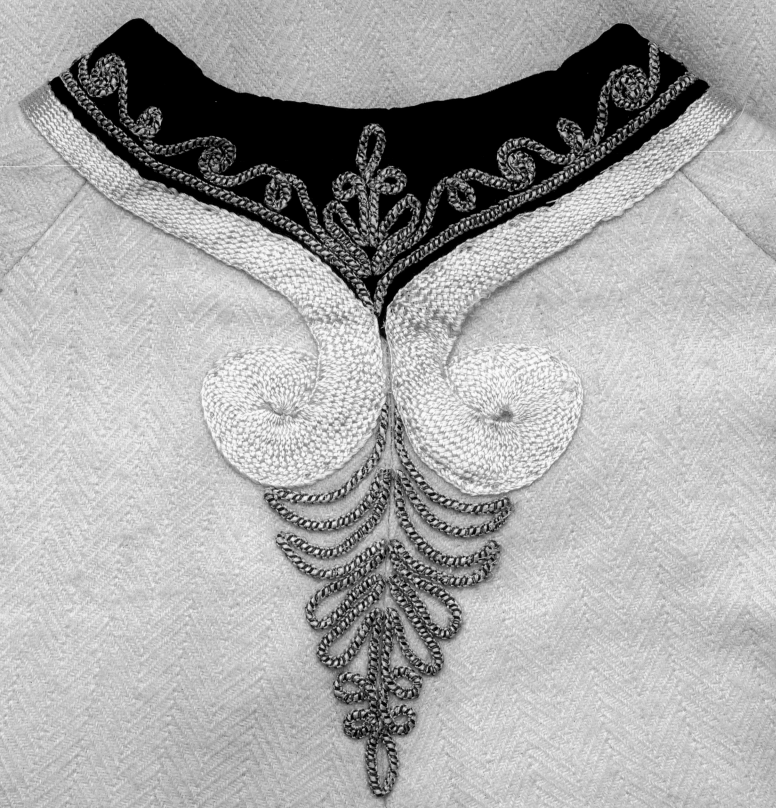

48. Coat, wool, about 1912
Coat of cream-coloured wool, herringbone weave, fully lined with white cotton sateen. Fastens down left side with three mother-of-pearl and gilt metal buttons, one now missing. Full sleeves with softly pleated headings and deep turn-back cuffs. Neckline and cuffs decorated with applied black cotton velvet, broad woven band of cream silk braid and narrower black and white silk braid.
Accession no. 1967.187.6

49. Coat, wool and rabbit fur, about 1925-30

Coat of maroon-coloured wool, fully lined with maroon-coloured silk. Loose fitting, fastening in centre front with one large plastic button at low waist level. Deep stand-up collar and cuffs of brindle-coloured rabbit fur.
Labelled *Cripps, Sons & Co., 12-14 & 16 BOLD STREET, LIVERPOOL*
Accession no. 1967.187.2

50. Evening coat, rayon silk, about 1925-30

Evening coat of black ribbed rayon silk. Decorated around lower half, from low waistline to above hem, and around cuffs with deep band of white cotton machine embroidery. Two long ties of black rayon silk with long silk fringes at neckline. Unlined. This coat has a matching evening dress of black rayon silk, decorated with the same white cotton machine embroidery (not illustrated. See Appendix, Evening Clothes, accession no. 1967.187. 40).
Accession no. 1967.187.41

Detail, Cat. no. 50.

51. Coat, wool velour and beaver fur, about 1926-30

Coat of black wool velour, lined with grey wool flannel and black rayon silk. Loose fitting, fastening on left side of low waistline with large plastic button. Deep stand-up collar, cuffs and trim to centre front and sides of hemline of black beaver fur. Labelled *Cripps, Sons & Co., 12-14 & 16 BOLD STREET, LIVERPOOL*

Accession no. WAG 2001.45.10

52. Coat, red sable, 1927

Coat of dyed red sable, also known as Kolinsky mink, worked in a chevron pattern, fully lined with olive green cotton sateen. Deep shawl collar and long cuffs. Fastens on the left side at low waist level with large sable button.

In original box, labelled *Bon Marché, Liverpool (Liverpool) Ltd, Mrs Tinnie* (sic), *Clayton Lodge, Aigburth Road, Liverpool, Assistant 420, check no. 9875, paid or X – 17/L, date 10/11/27*
Accession no. WAG 2001.45.5

53. Coat, wool facecloth and chinchilla fur, about 1927-30

Coat of black wool facecloth, fully lined with pale grey silk. Fastens on left side with large plastic button. Deep collar, single full-length rever and deep cuffs, all of grey chinchilla fur.
Labelled *G.H. Lee & Co. Ltd, Liverpool*
Accession no. WAG 2001.45.13

54. Coat, sealskin, 1928

Coat of black sealskin, fully lined with black silk and silk satin in a checkered weave. Fastens at left side with large brown celluloid button. Deep collar and cuffs.
Labelled *W. Creamer & Co., LADIES' TAILORS, 56 BOLD ST., LIVERPOOL, FURRIERS BY APPOINTMENT, H.M. ALEXANDRA,* and *STORAGE, Name Tinne, No. S3739, Date recd. 2/7/28*
Accession no. WAG 2001.45.4

55. Coat, silk ottoman and moleskin, about 1930

Coat of black silk ottoman, fully lined with pale grey rayon crepe in a quilted finish. Collar, full-length revers to hemline and deep cuffs all of brown moleskin.
Labelled *Cripps, Sons & Co., 12-14 & 16 BOLD STREET, LIVERPOOL*
Accession no. WAG 2001.45.15

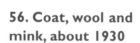

56. Coat, wool and mink, about 1930

Coat of black wool, with woven diagonal stripe, fully lined with black rayon silk. Fastens at left side with two large plastic buttons. Deep collar and cuff trims of mink.
Accession no. WAG 2001.45.14

57. Coat, Persian lamb and beaver fur, about 1930

Coat of Persian lamb, fully lined with black rayon silk. Fastens on left side at low waist level with large cotton thread-covered button. Deep shawl collar and cuffs of black beaver fur.

Accession no. WAG 2001.45.17

58. Coat, moleskin, 1930

Coat of diamond moleskin, originally fully lined with brown silk, now almost completely removed due to shattering. Fastens on left side with one moleskin-covered button. Deep shawl collar and turned-back cuffs.
In original box, labelled *From Lewis's Ltd, Ranelagh Street, Liverpool, Mrs Tinne, Clayton Lodge, Aigburth, date 15/3/30. Dept – Furs*
Accession no. WAG 2001.45.8

59. Coat, nutria fur, about 1930

Coat of brown nutria fur, fully lined with brown figured silk, worked in a geometric pattern, but now split in places. Fastens on left side at low waist level with large button of plastic and abalone shell. Deep stand-up collar and turned-back cuffs.

Labelled *G.H. Lee & Co. Ltd, Liverpool*

Accession no. WAG 2001.45.16

60. Coat, antelope and beaver fur, 1935

Coat of antelope, fully lined with figured brown rayon silk. Fastens on left side at low waist level with large plastic and mother-of-pearl button. Deep stand-up collar and cuffs of black beaver fur.

In original box labelled *Bon Marché (Lpool Ltd), The Fashion Store, Mrs Tinne, Clayton Lodge, Aigburth, Date 3/10/35*

Accession no. WAG 2001.45.18

61. Coat, sealskin and mink, about 1934-38

Coat of black sealskin, fully lined with figured brown rayon silk, worked in a stylised floral design. Fastens on left side with large sealskin button. Very deep shawl collar and deep cuffs of mink.

Accession no. WAG 2001.45.21

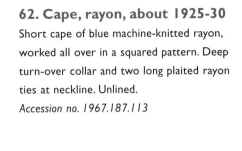

62. Cape, rayon, about 1925-30
Short cape of blue machine-knitted rayon,
worked all over in a squared pattern. Deep
turn-over collar and two long plaited rayon
ties at neckline. Unlined.
Accession no. 1967.187.113

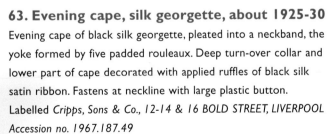

63. Evening cape, silk georgette, about 1925-30
Evening cape of black silk georgette, pleated into a neckband, the
yoke formed by five padded rouleaux. Deep turn-over collar and
lower part of cape decorated with applied ruffles of black silk
satin ribbon. Fastens at neckline with large plastic button.
Labelled *Cripps, Sons & Co., 12-14 & 16 BOLD STREET, LIVERPOOL*
Accession no. 1967.187.49

64. Shawl, silk velvet devoré, about 1925-30

Rectangular shawl, deep blue silk velvet devoré on a black silk crepe
ground, worked in a 'leaf' design, radiating out from the centre.
Decorated all around the edge with long knotted black silk fringe.
Accession no. 1967.187.100

65. Evening shoulder cape, cotton velvet, about 1930-34

Evening shoulder cape of black cotton velvet, fastening at centre front with a loop-through tie. Decorated all over with applied clear glass beads. Unlined.
Labelled *39/6, BL, 00/-, NR*
Accession no. WAG 2001.45.27

66. Evening coat, silk velvet and angora rabbit fur, about 1930-36

Evening coat of black silk velvet, fully lined with white silk crepe de chine. Very wide pagoda sleeves, very deep shawl collar of white angora rabbit fur. Fastens at centre front with one large plastic button.
Labelled *G.H. Lee & Co. Ltd, Liverpool*
In original box, marked and labelled *George Henry Lee & Co. Ltd, Basnett Street, Liverpool*
Accession no. WAG 2001.45.22

67. Evening mantle, silk crepe de chine and marabou feathers, about 1930

Evening mantle of black silk crepe de chine. Trimmed around all edges, armholes and the deep shawl collar with black marabou feathers. Unlined.
Accession no. WAG 2001.45.12

73

68. Bridge coat, silk velvet devoré and rabbit fur, about 1927-30

Bridge coat of pink and blue silk velvet devoré, worked in a floral pattern, fully lined with pink silk. Collar of dyed rabbit fur. Wraps over in centre front and fastens with tie belt at low waist level.

Accession no. WAG 2001.45.25

69. Bridge coat, silk velvet devoré and rabbit fur, about 1927-30

Bridge coat of royal blue silk velvet devoré, worked in a floral pattern, fully lined with royal blue silk. Collar of dyed rabbit fur. Wraps over in centre front and fastens with tie belt at low waist level. Small corsage of artificial flowers attached to rever on right-hand side.

Accession no. WAG 2001.45.24

70. Bridge coat, silk panne velvet and rabbit fur, about 1930-34

Bridge coat of black silk panne velvet printed with stylised palm leaf design in green and white. Fully lined with black silk chiffon. Scalloped bottom edge and cuffs. Collar of dyed rabbit fur. Fastens on left side with one large velvet-covered button.

Accession no. WAG 2001.45.26

71. Coat, wool crepe, about 1938-45

Coat of black wool crepe, fully lined with black rayon silk.
Edge-to-edge fastening at centre front with three metal
clips. Padded shoulders and slightly flared sleeves with
gathered headings. Decorated around neckline, cuffs and
down front with machine-embroidered leaves in black silk.
Accession no. 1967.187.111

72. Stole, squirrel fur and sable tails, about 1910-15

Stole of grey squirrel fur, trimmed with dark brown sable
tails at each end and backed with grey-brown silk.
In (original?) box marked *Owen Owen Ltd, Liverpool*
Labelled *MR/MD 4728, 20 gns* (20 guineas)
Possibly one of a pair of stoles, together with WAG
2003.45.48, not illustrated. See Appendix, Outdoor Clothes
and Furs. Such stoles were sometimes sold in pairs
Accession no. WAG 2001.45.47

73. Stole, ermine and silk satin, about 1910-20

Broad stole of ermine, backed with white silk satin, trimmed with ermine tails at both ends. In original (?) box marked *Marten and Co., Furriers and Skin Merchants, 40 Bold Street, Liverpool, and at 235 Lord Street, Southport*
Accession no. WAG 2001.45.49

74. Stole, moleskin and rayon silk, 1926

Broad stole of brown diamond moleskin, backed with figured brown rayon silk. Small ruched-top pocket attached to backing. Plastic link fastener with brown silk-covered bobble at each end. Original receipt, dated 22 October 1926, from the Bon Marché, Church Street, Liverpool, still survives. Stole cost £9.9.0
Accession no. WAG 2001.45.37

75. Stole, moleskin and silk, 1926

Stole of brown moleskin, backed with plain brown silk. Fastens with brown silk link cord and hook. Original receipt, dated 22 October 1926, from the Bon Marché, Church Street, Liverpool, still survives. Stole cost £8.8.0
Accession no. WAG 2001.45.38

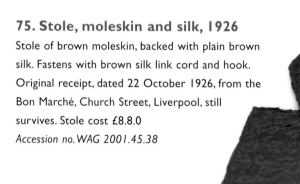

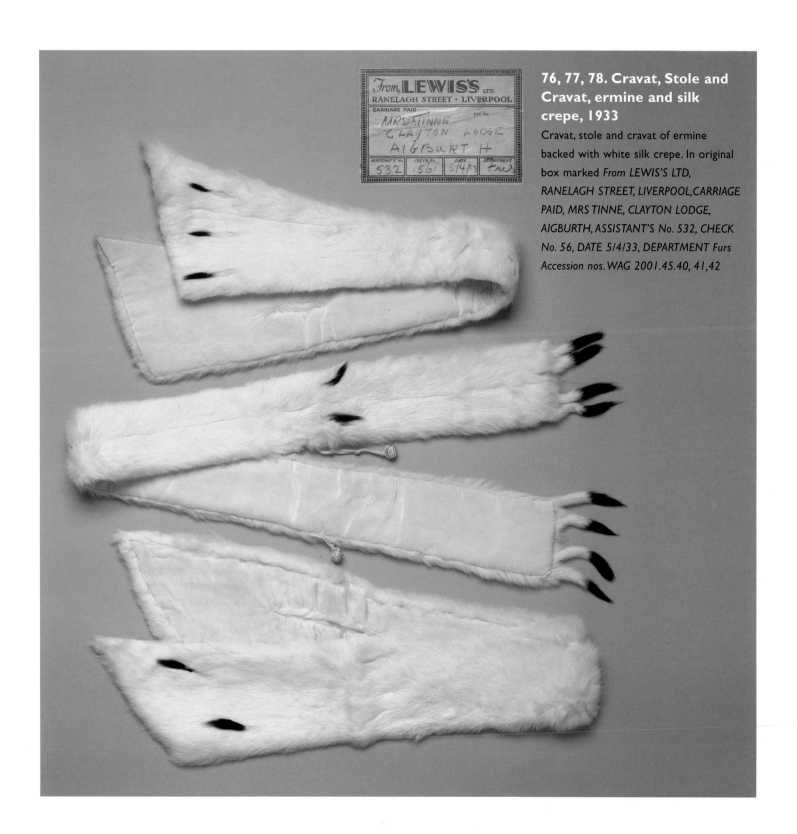

76, 77, 78. Cravat, Stole and Cravat, ermine and silk crepe, 1933

Cravat, stole and cravat of ermine backed with white silk crepe. In original box marked *From LEWIS'S LTD, RANELAGH STREET, LIVERPOOL, CARRIAGE PAID, MRS TINNE, CLAYTON LODGE, AIGBURTH, ASSISTANT'S No. 532, CHECK No. 56, DATE 5/4/33, DEPARTMENT Furs* Accession nos. WAG 2001.45.40, 41,42

79 & 80. Stoles, mink and rayon silk, about 1930-35

Long narrow stoles of mink, both backed with brown rayon silk. Both
fasten with brown silk link cord and hook. Sable fur tails.

In (original?) box marked *Owen Owen Ltd, Liverpool*

Accession no. WAG 2001.45.33, 34

81. Stole, silver fox fur and silk velvet, about 1930-35

Stole, double silver fox fur, joined together at single mask, backed with black silk velvet. Fastens with brown silk link cord and hook.

Labelled *120, R/T/R, 8.8.0 (8 guineas)*, *SILVER FOX*

Accession no. WAG 2001.45.31

82. Stole, winter fox fur and silk satin, about 1930-35

Stole of white winter fox fur backed with white silk satin.

In same, original, box as Cat. no. 73, WAG 2001.45.49, marked *Marten & Co., Furriers and Skin Merchants, 40 Bold Street, Liverpool, and at 235 Lord Street, Southport*

Accession no. WAG 2001.45.50

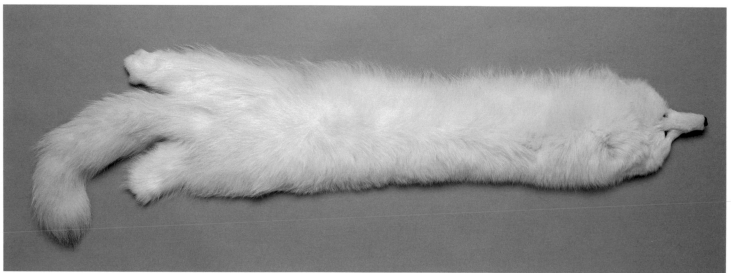

79

BLOUSES

83. Blouse, cotton muslin, about 1910-20

Blouse of white cotton muslin, the turned-over collar, cuffs, shoulders and centre front all decorated with inserts of machine-made drawn threadwork and floral whitework embroidery. Fastens down centre front with row of nine cotton crochet-covered buttons and hook and eye. Elasticated waistline.

Labelled *48*

Accession no. WAG 2001.45.161

84. Blouse, cotton muslin, about 1910-20

Blouse of white cotton muslin, with small turned-over collar edged with machine-made Valenciennes lace. Fastens down centre back with row of cotton-covered buttons. Yoke and centre front decorated with floral whitework embroidery, crocheted in-fills and a tape lace insert. Long plain sleeves and cuffs. Vertical pin-tucks to sides and centre back. Elasticated waistline.

Labelled *AVA, 46*

Accession no. 1967.187.123

85. Blouse, cotton muslin, about 1910-20

Blouse of white cotton muslin, with small turned-over collar edged with machine-made Valenciennes lace. Fastens down centre back with row of cotton-covered buttons. Yoke and centre front decorated with floral whitework embroidery, cutwork and circular crocheted inserts. Long plain sleeves and cuffs, with mother-of-pearl cufflinks. Vertical pin-tucks to sides of yoke and centre back. Elasticated waistline.

Labelled *AVA, 46*

Accession no. 1967.187.115

86. Blouse, cotton muslin, about 1910-20

Blouse of white cotton muslin, with scallop-edged turned-over collar and revers. Fastens down centre front with hooks and eyes, disguised by two groups of small white cotton bobbles. Centre front, collar and cuffs all decorated with floral whitework embroidery. Faggoting detail to yoke and tops of sleeves.

Labelled *14?* and *12/11*

Accession no. WAG 2001.45.54

87. Blouse, cotton muslin, about 1910-20

Blouse of white cotton muslin, the turned-over collar and deep cuffs decorated with floral whitework embroidery. Fastens down centre front with three cotton crochet-covered buttons. Back and front decorated with machine-made drawn threadwork inserts, worked in a geometric pattern. Panels of floral whitework embroidery to sides and centre front.

Labelled *No. 1484, Size 14?, Mach'st 36, Finisher G, Order*

Accession no. WAG 2001.45.57

88. Blouse, cotton muslin, about 1910-20

Blouse of ivory-coloured cotton muslin, with cross-over front and shawl collar, edged with machine-made torchon lace. Long sleeves, the cuffs also edged with machine-made torchon lace. Vertical pin-tucks and faggoting detail to shoulders. Collar decorated with circular crocheted inserts. Labelled *Harrod's Ltd, LONDON, S.W, BLOUSE & SKIRT DEPT. Accession no. 1967.187.121*

89. Blouse, cotton muslin, about 1916

Blouse of white cotton muslin, with deep turned-over collar edged with machine-made Valenciennes lace. Fastens down centre front with five mother-of-pearl buttons. Three quarter-length sleeves with turned-back cuffs edged with machine-made Valenciennes lace. Shoulders and sleeves decorated with whitework embroidery in stylised leaf pattern. Elasticated waistline.

Emily is pictured wearing this blouse in the family photograph, opposite, which includes her baby daughter Bertha who was born in February 1916.

Labelled *AVA, 42*

Accession no. 1967.187.122

90. Blouse, cotton muslin, about 1910-20

Blouse of white cotton muslin, the round neckline decorated with a ruffle of machine-made Valenciennes lace. Fastens down centre front with six buttons, all now missing. Long plain sleeves and cuffs. Yoke decorated with diamond-shaped crocheted inserts, centre front decorated with floral whitework embroidery. Elasticated waistline.
Labelled AVA, 44
Accession no. 1967.187.114

91. Blouse, cotton muslin, about 1910-20

Blouse of white cotton muslin, the deep turned-over collar edged with machine-made Valenciennes lace. Fastens down centre front with row of tiny buttons and loops, concealed behind row of larger cotton crochet-covered buttons. Long sleeves, the turned-back cuffs decorated with inserts of machine-made Valenciennes lace. Centre front decorated with vertical pin-tucks, drawn threadwork and whitework embroidery.
Labelled PARIS MODEL and AVA, 48. Paper label at bottom edge marked HAND MADE BLOUSES, MARQUE AVA, No. 7287, MADE IN FRANCE, 2gns (2 guineas)
Accession no. WAG 2001.45.55

92. Blouse, silk, about 1910-20

Blouse of ivory-coloured silk, the rounded neckline with square-cut turned-over collar and mother-of-pearl buttons. Three quarter-length sleeves with square-cut turned-back cuffs and mother-of-pearl buttons. Fastens with hooks and eyes down centre back. Front and back both decorated with panels of vertical pin-tucks.
Labelled SIZE 1, The St. Margaret, REGD.
Accession no. 1967.187.117

93. Blouse, cotton lawn and silk chiffon, about 1913

Blouse of white cotton lawn, with small warp-printed floral pattern in pale pink, pale blue and green, covered with a layer of brown silk chiffon. Turned-over collar of white silk chiffon, machine-embroidered with pale blue silk roses and decorative edging. Centre front hook and eye fastenings hidden by jabot of accordion-pleated brown silk chiffon. Pleated silk chiffon cuffs. Elasticated waistline.

Emily is pictured wearing this blouse in a family photograph which includes her eldest daughter, Elspeth (1911-2000), aged about two.

Accession no. 1967.187.118

94. Blouse, cotton net and silk chiffon, about 1913-15

Blouse of double-layered white cotton net, covered with layer of dark green silk chiffon. Turned-over collar of machine-embroidered net with scalloped edge. Fastens down centre front with hooks and eyes behind row of tiny mother-of-pearl buttons and vertical bands of scallop-edged machine-embroidered net. The edges of the outer layer of silk chiffon are decorated with multi-coloured machine embroidery. Long sleeves and silk chiffon cuffs with pointed edges. Elasticated waistline.
Accession no. 1967.187.120

95. Blouse, cotton net and silk chiffon, about 1913-15

Blouse of double-layered white cotton net, covered with layer of navy blue silk chiffon. Turned-over collar of machine-embroidered net with scalloped edge. Fastens down centre front with hooks and eyes concealed by row of tiny silk-covered buttons and vertical bands of machine-embroidered net. The edges of the outer layer of silk chiffon are decorated with machine-embroidered floral wreaths in pink, blue and green. Long sleeves and silk chiffon cuffs with pointed edges. Elasticated waistline.

Accession no. 1967.187.119

96. Blouse, silk crepe de chine, about 1933-35

Blouse of white silk crepe de chine, with wide neckline opening to a V-shape at centre front. Decorated down centre front and sleeves with floral silk hand-embroidery in red, blue, yellow, orange, green and brown. Neckline, cuffs and bottom edge are all smocked and worked with the same coloured silks.

Labelled *HAND EMBROIDERY, MADE IN HUNGARY*

This blouse was worn by Emily Tinne's youngest daughter, Alexine (1923-2011) as a young girl of 10-12.

Accession no. WAG 2001.45.58

OWEN OWEN,
LTD.

13/6

LIVERPOOL.

UNDERWEAR
AND NIGHTWEAR

97. Petticoat, cotton, about 1910-20

Full-length white cotton petticoat, with square neckline, no sleeves. Yoke decorated with inserted band of whitework embroidery, and with broderie anglaise around neckline and armholes. Lower part of skirt decorated with alternating bands of horizontal pin-tucks and inserted whitework embroidery. Fastens down centre back with row of linen-covered buttons.

Labelled *E.M. Tinne*

Accession no. 1967.187.362

98. Petticoat, cotton, about 1920-30

Full-length white cotton petticoat, with square-cut bodice top and narrow shoulder straps. Dropped waistline, the skirt gathered into narrow pleats at either side, over hips. Decorated across centre front of bodice and above hemline with faggoting and embroidered floral cutwork.

Labelled *No.14716, 48, MADE IN FRANCE* and *G.H. LEE & Co. LTD, LIVERPOOL, U.G., BRITISH AND FRENCH LINGERIE & BABY LINEN, 7/11*

Accession no. 1967.187.407

99. Open-leg drawers, cotton, about 1900-20

Pair of white cotton open-leg drawers, fastening at centre back with a narrow drawstring tape. Decorated around the legs with deep band of broderie anglaise, with pointed edge, and with inserted ribbon of pale green silk satin, tied in a bow on each leg.

Accession no. 1967.187.354

100. Combinations, cotton, about 1910-20

Pair of white cotton combinations, fastening down centre front with row of linen-covered buttons. Buttoned flap at centre back. Square-cut neckline decorated with band of floral embroidery in pale blue and white and trimmed around edges and at armholes with crocheted lace. Legs decorated with band of pale blue and white floral embroidery and crocheted edging.

Accession no. 1967.187.356

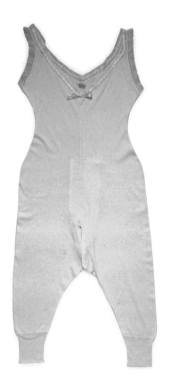

101. Combinations, cotton, about 1930-40

Pair of cream-coloured machine-knitted cotton combinations, fitted to shape of body. V-shaped neckline, armholes and shoulder straps edged with machine-made lace border. Neckline also laced with narrow knitted silk ribbon, with small bow at centre front. Cross-over flap opening at centre back. Elasticated ankle cuffs. Labelled *QUALITY E, "MERIDIAN", INTERLOCK REGD., BRITISH MAKE.* Made by J.B. Lewis & Sons of Nottingham

Accession no. 1967.187.357

102. Camisole, cotton, about 1905-15

White cotton camisole, the fly-fastening to centre front concealing row of tiny buttons. Square-shaped neckline and armholes edged with machine-made lace, the yoke decorated with band of whitework embroidery and inserted bands of machine-made lace. Neckline threaded with narrow pale pink silk ribbon. Drawstring through waistline, with row of flat, narrow vertical pleats forming pouched effect to centre front of bodice.
Accession no. 1967.187.340

103. Camisole, cotton lawn, about 1910-20

White cotton lawn camisole, the fly-fastening to centre back concealing row of tiny mother-of-pearl buttons. Wide scoop neckline and armholes both decorated with torchon lace edging, threaded with narrow pale pink silk satin ribbon. Centre front of bodice decorated with torchon lace inserts and whitework embroidery. Narrow pale pink silk ribbon threaded through waistline. Vertical pin-tucks to centre of bodice, above waistline.
Labelled *OWEN OWEN LTD, LIVERPOOL, 12/6D*
Accession no. 1967.187.482

104. Camisole, silk, about 1910-20

White silk camisole, fastening down centre front with row of tiny linen-covered buttons. Wide scooped neckline and armholes both decorated with machine-made lace threaded with pale green silk ribbon. Bodice gathered into narrow white cotton waistband, fastening at centre front with hook and eye.
Accession no. 1967.187.345

105. Camisole, cotton, about 1910-20

White cotton camisole, slightly fitted to the body, fastening down centre front with row of mother-of-pearl buttons. Square-shaped neckline and armholes edged with machine-made lace and narrow feather-stitched tape. Neckline decorated with inserted band of machine-made lace and threaded with narrow white cotton drawstring tape. Bands of vertical pin-tucks to centre front and sides of bodice. Drawstring to back of waistline.
Accession no. 1967.187.342

106. Camisole, cotton, about 1910-20

Pale pink cotton camisole, the fly-fastening to centre front concealing two tiny mother-of-pearl buttons. Wide V-shaped neckline, decorated with deep band of machine-made Valenciennes lace threaded with narrow pale pink silk ribbon. Short sleeves decorated with inserts and edging of machine-made lace. Intersecting lace inserts across bodice front form diamond pattern. Cotton tape drawstring through waistline.
Labelled *OWEN OWEN LTD, LIVERPOOL, 6/11*
Accession no. 1967.187.485

107. Camisole, cotton, about 1920

White cotton camisole, the fly-fastening to centre front concealing the row of tiny mother-of-pearl buttons. Square-cut bodice top with shoulder straps of machine-made lace, and horizontal inserts of machine-made lace. Bodice front composed of alternating bands of vertical pin-tucks and machine-made lace inserts. Plain cotton waistband.
Labelled *E.M. Tinne* in red, and inscribed *E.M. Tinne* in black ink
Accession no. WAG 2001.45.64

108. Camisole, cotton, about 1920-30

White cotton camisole, plain rectangular shape, with narrow shoulder straps. Scalloped and embroidered edges to top, bottom and shoulder straps. Narrow pale pink silk ribbon threaded through top edge. Decorated at centre top with circular floral motif in cutwork and whitework embroidery. Elasticated at both sides, the elastic now perished.
Labelled *G.H. LEE & Co. LTD, LIVERPOOL, U.G., BRITISH & FRENCH LINGERIE & BABY LINEN, price 4/9*, and *G.H. LEE & Co. LTD, LIVERPOOL, BRITISH & FRENCH LINGERIE & BABY LINEN, price 5/6*
Accession no. 1967.187.343

109. Bust bodice, cotton, about 1920

White cotton bust bodice, front fastening with four white glass buttons. Wide, V-shaped neckline, shoulder straps of elasticated cotton, now perished. Bodice front sewn with narrow strips of white cotton, crossing over each other to produce a checked pattern. Elasticated cotton band at waistline. Boned and laced up centre back.
Accession no. 1967.187.348.

110. Brassière, cotton and machine-made lace, about 1920-25

Brassière composed of four triangles of white cotton broderie anglaise, two at back and two at front, joined to deep bands of machine-made lace with scalloped edging. Front fastening with hooks and eyes behind a fly front. Wide, V-shaped neckline threaded with narrow pale pink silk ribbon, finishing in a bow at centre front. Narrow tape at centre front to attach to corset with metal hook, the hook now missing.
Stamped *BIEN JOLIE BRASSIERE, MADE IN U.S.A., 15090, 40*
Made by Benjamin & Johnes, U.S.A.
Accession no. 1967.187.347

111. Brassière, cotton, about 1920-25

White cotton brassière, front fastening with hooks and eyes behind a fly front. Wide, shallow neckline, decorated at front and back with band of broderie anglaise in a floral and geometric design. Broderie anglaise shoulder straps, decorated with scallop-edged white cotton tape. Narrow tape at centre front to attach to corset with metal hook, the hook now missing.

Stamped *BIEN JOLIE BRASSIERE, MADE IN U.S.A., 5079, 42*

Made by Benjamin & Johnes, U.S.A.

Accession no. 1967.187.350

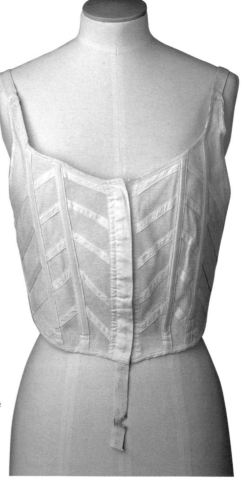

112. Brassière, cotton and cotton net, about 1920-25

Brassière of white elasticated cotton net, over-sewn with narrow bands of white cotton, some of them boned, in a chevron pattern. Front fastening with hooks and eyes behind a fly front. Wide, scooped neckline, shoulder straps of elasticated cotton, now perished. Laces up centre back. Elasticated bands at sides. Narrow tape at centre front to attach to corset with metal hook, the hook now missing.

Stamped *BIEN JOLIE BRASSIERE, MADE IN U.S.A., 48/3, 36*

Made by Benjamin & Johnes, U.S.A.

Accession no. 1967.187.349

113. Corset, cotton net, about 1900-05

Corset of white cotton net, lightly boned, possibly worn for playing sport. Cut low under breasts and high over hips for greater flexibility. Decorated at top and bottom edges with ruffle of broderie anglaise and in centre front with ivory silk satin bow. Four metal fastenings to busk down centre front, laces up centre back. Two elasticated suspenders attached at centre front.

Possibly worn by Emily Tinne as a teenager.

Inscribed *1414, 3* in pencil

Accession no. WAG 2001.45.66

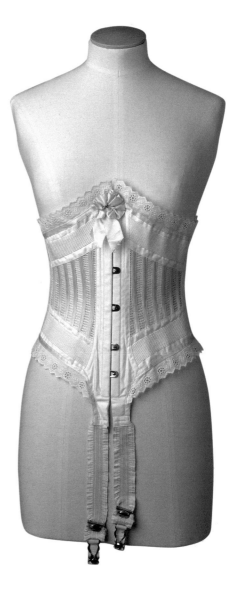

114. Maternity corset, cotton twill, about 1920

Maternity corset of white cotton twill, with elasticated panels inserted at either side of central busk. Decorated around top edge with band of broderie anglaise. Laces up centre back and both sides, to allow for development of pregnancy. Two elasticated suspenders attached to bottom edge.

Stamped *La Mère* and *British Make*

Other maternity clothes survive in the collection. See Cat. no.1, and Appendix, Day Clothes, accession no. 1967.187.19

Accession no. WAG 2003.11.4

115. Nightdress, cotton, about 1910-20

Full-length white cotton nightdress, with rounded neckline and turned-over collar. Collar, front placket and turned-back cuffs all edged with ruffles of broderie anglaise and white feather stitch embroidery. Placket conceals front fastening with small mother-of-pearl buttons. Band of vertical pin-tucks to bodice front, either side of central placket.
Accession no. 1967.187.376

116. Dressing gown, cotton, about 1910-20

Full-length dressing gown of white figured cotton, woven all over with a spot motif. Deep, cross-over shawl collar and cuffs decorated with broderie anglaise inserts and deep gathered ruffles. Fastens on left side with hooks and eyes. Two deep, horizontal pleats at hemline. Unlined.
Accession no. 1967.187.381

117. Bed jacket, cotton lawn, about 1910-20

White cotton lawn bed jacket, cut in a basic T-shape, with small gores beneath the arms. Rounded neckline, fastening on left side of neck with small, single white glass button. Wide, elbow-length sleeves. Neckline, centre front edges and cuffs all decorated with band of broderie anglaise and feather stitch embroidery, and edged with ruffle of machine-made lace.

Labelled *E.M. Tinne*

Accession no. 1967.187.379

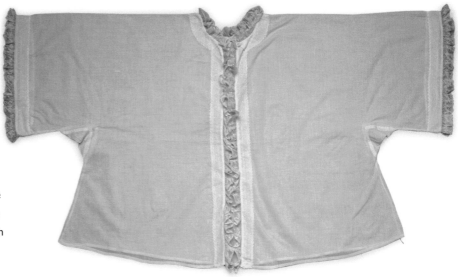

118. Bed jacket, cotton, about 1910-20

White cotton bed jacket, with A-line shaped body and squared neckline. Wrap-over front, fastening high up on right side with small mother-of-pearl button. Full-length, slightly puffed sleeves. Neckline, front edges and cuffs all edged with band of broderie anglaise and narrow ruffle of machine-made lace.

Labelled *E.M. Tinne*

Accession no. 1967.187.378

SWIMWEAR

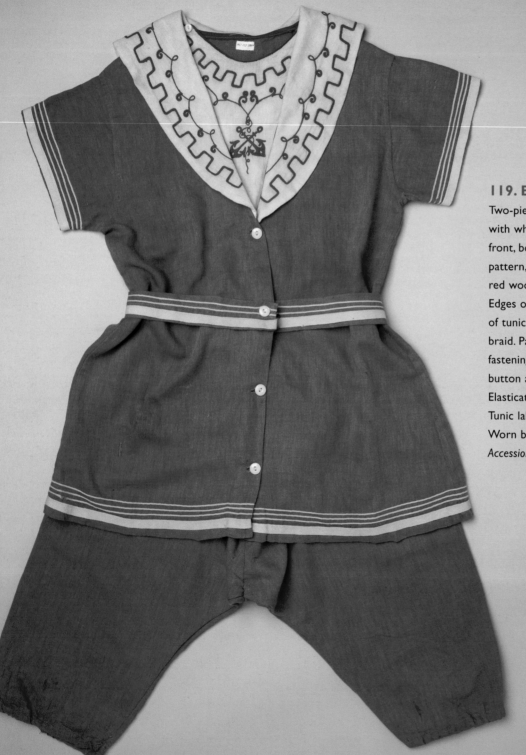

119. Bathing costume, wool serge, 1910

Two-piece bathing costume of red-orange wool serge. Tunic with white wool serge sailor collar and buttoned-in bib-front, both embroidered with scrolling design and Greek key pattern, and with pair of crossed anchors in centre front, in red wool. Front fastening with four white glass buttons. Edges of the short sleeves, separate belt and bottom edge of tunic all decorated with applied bands of white woollen braid. Pair of matching knee-length bathing knickers, fastening at either side of waistline with single white glass button and at centre back with cotton drawstring. Elasticated knees, the elastic now perished.

Tunic labelled *L.Y. & J. Nathan, 4 Hardman Street, Liverpool*

Worn by Emily Tinne during her honeymoon in Ireland, 1910

Accession no. 1967.187.388a & 388b

120. Bathing cap, rubberised cotton sateen, 1910

Bathing cap of orange cotton sateen, backed with a rubber solution to make it waterproof. Shallow crown gathered into band around forehead, decorated at centre front with three horizontal pleats of cream silk, and at each side with a cotton sateen rosette. Can be adjusted to head size by means of red woollen drawstring tape at centre back. Made to match bathing costume opposite.

Accession no. 1967.187.388c

121. Pair of espadrilles, linen and wool, 1910

Pair of espadrilles, white linen, the soles of coiled jute, the edges bound with faded pink cotton tape. Laces of faded pink cotton. Front and back of uppers embroidered with an anchor motif in red wool. Made to match bathing costume and bathing cap, above.

Accession no. 1967.187.388d

122. Bathing costume, cotton jersey, about 1915-20

Bathing costume of navy blue machine-knitted cotton jersey. V-shaped neckline and edging bands to armholes, legs and bottom of short overskirt all of yellow cotton jersey. Legs attached from waistline, beneath overskirt. Fastens with two buttons on left shoulder.

Accession no. 1967.187.383

123. Bathing costume, cotton jersey, about 1920-25

Bathing costume of navy blue machine-knitted cotton jersey. Scooped neckline, armholes and edges of legs all of white knitted cotton jersey. Fastens with two buttons on left shoulder.

Accession no. 1967.187.385

124. Bathing costume, cotton jersey, about 1925-30

Bathing costume of black machine-knitted cotton jersey, with vest-like top section and short legs. Top half of costume is divided diagonally, the left side worked in blue and yellow horizontal stripes. Fastens with two mother-of-pearl buttons on left shoulder. Belt loops at hip level but belt now missing. Labelled *MERIDIAN REGD, INTERLOCK, THE PERFECT FABRIC FOR SENSITIVE SKINS, BRITISH MAKE, AFTER BATHING RINSE WELL IN CLEAR FRESH WATER, RESTORE TO NORMAL SHAPE BEFORE DRYING. Sensola*
Made by J.B. Lewis & Sons of Nottingham
Accession no. 1967.187.387

SHOES

**125. Pair of shoes, glacé kid
leather, about 1910-15**
Pair of black glacé kid leather shoes, with
high vamps and small tongues. Decorated
on the vamps with oval-shaped gilt metal
buckles, set with diamanté pastes. Pointed
toes and kid-covered Louis heels.
Stamped *Made in Paris for W.H. Watts & Co.
Ltd, Boot & Shoe Importers, Liverpool*
Accession no. 1967.187.233

126. Pair of shoes, glacé kid leather, about 1910-15

Pair of black glacé kid leather shoes, with pointed toes and patent leather-covered Louis heels. Fastening across instep with double strap and two buttons. Cut-away vamps, decorated with applied black glass beads. Insoles of bright pink silk satin.
Accession no. 1967.187.226

127. Pair of shoes, glacé kid leather, about 1910-15

Pair of dark brown glacé kid leather shoes, with pointed toes and kid-covered Louis heels. Fastening across instep with strap and button. Decorated across vamps and ankle straps with applied cut steel and bronze beads, the steel beads now rusting and turning brown. Insoles of pale blue silk satin.
Stamped The Imperial, Regd. No. 48340
Accession no. 1967.187.225

128. Pair of shoes, glacé kid leather, about 1910-15

Pair of black glacé kid leather court shoes, with pointed toes, kid-covered Louis heels and black silk petersham ribbon bows on the vamps.
Stamped J. Collinson & Co., 34 & 36 BOLD ST, LIVERPOOL
Accession no. 1967.187.228

129. Pair of shoes, leather, about 1915-20

Pair of black leather shoes, with pointed toes, patent leather-covered
Louis heels and elasticated side vents. Cut-away vamps, forming two
sets of crossed straps on each one. Decorated with three small oval-
shaped buckles of cut steel on each vamp.

Accession no. 1967.187.221

130. Pair of shoes, suede, about 1915-20

Pair of black suede shoes, with pointed toes, elasticated
side vents and suede-covered heels. Cut-away vamps,
forming four narrow straps across the fronts. Decorated
with five applied rosettes of cut-steel beads.
Labelled *NORVIC, THE SHOE DE LUXE* and stamped
NORVIC, SHOES FOR LADIES on the leather soles
Made by Howlett and White, Norwich.

Accession no. 1967.187.224

131. Pair of boots, leather, about 1910-20

Pair of black leather lace-up boots, with pointed toes and brogue
slips, stacked leather heels. Lacing up centre front of ankles.

Accession no. 1967.187.216

132. Pair of shoes, glacé kid leather, about 1920

Pair of black glacé kid leather shoes with pointed toes, leather-covered Cuban heels, and high tongues decorated with large cut steel buckles.
Stamped *NORVIC* inside and *NORVIC, SHOES FOR LADIES, CASH PRICE 32/6* on the leather soles
Made by Howlett and White, Norwich.
Accession no. 1967.187.217

133. Pair of shoes, glacé kid leather, about 1920

Pair of black glacé kid leather shoes, with pointed toes, low kid-covered Cuban heels, and shaped tongues decorated with oval-shaped pierced metal buckles, set with cut steel beads. Tongue conceals strap and button fastening in each shoe.
In original shoebox, labelled *LOTUS, BRITISH MADE, Glacé Black Kid, 6¹/₂ MIDFORM* and *Delta Shoes, Lotus Shoes*
Stamped *LOTUS MIDFORM, BRITISH MADE*
Made by Lotus Shoes, Stafford
Accession no. 1967.187.223 & 223a

134. Pair of shoes, leather, about 1923-26
Pair of tan-coloured leather shoes, with long pointed toes and narrow brogue slips, strap and button across insteps, and stacked leather Louis heels.
Stamped *J. Collinson & Co., Bold Street, Liverpool, Chester, Wrexham*
Accession no. 1967.187.220

135. Pair of shoes, cotton sateen, about 1923-26
Pair of black cotton sateen evening shoes, with long pointed toes and strap and button across insteps, the button set with diamanté pastes. Sateen-covered Louis heels.
Labelled *Thierry, est. 1839, Military Bootmaker, Bold Street, Liverpool* and stamped *G. Thièrry, 5 Bold Street, Liverpool*
Accession no. 1967.187.230

136. Pair of shoes, patent leather, about 1934

Pair of black patent leather shoes, with pointed toes and patent leather-covered Louis heels. Strap and button across insteps, the vamps edged with strip of pinky-brown punched leather. Stamped *Helen* on the leather sole, and labelled *9.34, 8/11*
Accession no. 1967.187.218

137. Pair of shoes, leather, about 1930-34
Pair of grey leather shoes, with pointed toes, strap and button across the insteps and leather-covered Louis heels. Decorated across vamps and quarters with applied narrow strips of pale pink leather and with decorative stitching.
Accession no. 1967.187.219

138. Pair of shoes, wool gabardine, about 1930-32
Pair of black wool gabardine court shoes, with pointed toes and gabardine-covered Cuban heels. Decorated on the vamps with small pewter buckles, with gabardine centres, set with diamanté pastes. Insoles of purple silk satin.
Accession no. 1967.187.232

139. Pair of shoes, patent leather, about 1932-36

Pair of brown patent leather shoes, with pointed toes, high vamps
and pleated tongues, trimmed with narrow lizard skin straps and
small metal buckles. Patent leather-covered heels.

Stamped *LEWIS'S, LIVERPOOL, MANCHESTER, LEEDS, BIRMINGHAM,
GLASGOW* and *NON-SLIP HEELS*

Accession no. WAG 2003.11.10

140. Pair of shoes, leather, about 1935-40

Pair of brown leather lace-up shoes, with pointed toes and stacked
leather Cuban heels. Small stamped leather inserts to the facings.

Stamped *Begonia Shoe* on the leather soles

Accession no. WAG 2003.11.8

HATS

141. Sun bonnet, cotton, about 1900-15
Pale blue cotton sun bonnet, machine-stitched, the crown and brim both shaped by cording. Gathered neck-shield stitched to the back of crown. Two cotton ties.
Accession no. 1967.187.204

142. Motoring bonnet, sealskin and silk chiffon, about 1910-15

Motoring bonnet of sealskin lined with dark brown silk satin, with long veil of dark brown silk chiffon attached across the front and down the right-hand side. Large applied rosette of printed cotton over each ear, formed from separate petals, each one covered with a fine layer of black silk chiffon. Wide ribbons of dark brown silk faille. Brown knitted woollen stocking pinned into centre back of lining to hold the wearer's hair in place beneath bonnet.
Accession no. WAG 2001.45.45

143. Hat, silk velour, about 1918-22

Hat of black silk velour, with deep rounded crown, lined with black silk, and elliptical-shaped brim, the edge bound with black silk petersham ribbon. Deep band of black silk velour around the crown, narrower band of black petersham ribbon and dyed black ostrich feather around brim.
Labelled *Madame Val Smith Ltd, Liverpool*
Accession no. 1976.187.257

144. Hat, silk net, about 1918-22

Hat of black silk net, with deep rounded crown, lined with black silk. Wire frame brim, covered with black silk net and edged with gathered band of black silk petersham ribbon. Crown decorated with large ruffled rosette of petersham-edged black silk net.
Accession no. 1967.187.261

113

145. Hat, silk velour, about 1918-22

Hat of black silk velour, with deep rounded crown, lined with black silk. Wide velour brim, turned up at the back. Crown decorated with curled, glossy black egret feathers.

Labelled *Millinery Bon Marché, (Liverpool) Ltd*

Accession no. 1967.187.250

146. Hat, wool crepe, about 1922-24

Hat of coffee-coloured wool crepe, with deep rounded crown and elliptical-shaped brim, turned up at the left-hand side. Underside of brim decorated with narrow bands of ruched coffee-coloured silk ribbon, applied in concentric semi-circles. Crown lined with black cotton sateen.

Accession no. 1967.187.334

147. Hat, horsehair, about 1924-26

Hat of woven black horsehair, known as crin, with deep crown, higher at the front than the back. Narrow brim of woven crin, the edge bound with black silk satin. Crown decorated with two narrow bands of black silk satin and applied egret feathers. Crown lined with black silk.

Labelled *George Henry Lee & Co. Ltd, Basnett Street, Liverpool*

Accession no. 1967.187.258

148. Hat, silk satin and straw, about 1924-26

Hat of woven black straw, the deep crown covered with swathed and folded black silk satin. Narrow brim of woven straw, turned up at the back. Centre front of crown decorated with three triangular-shaped pieces of black corded silk, each edged with woven black horsehair, known as crin. Triangular white metal brooch to left-hand side of crown. Lined with black silk.
Accession no. 1967.187.285

149. Hat, silk velour, about 1924-26

Hat of black silk velour, with deep crown and fairly narrow brim, turned up at the back. Crown decorated with deep, swathed band of black silk velvet and with pleated rosettes of shiny black silk ribbon. Large circular ribbon rosette to left-hand side, the centre set with tiny silver metal studs. Crown lined with black silk.
Accession no. 1967.187.286

150. Hat, horsehair, about 1925-27

Hat of woven black horsehair, known as crin, the deep circular crown lined with black silk. Brim of woven crin, the wired edge bound with black silk satin. Crown decorated with band of black silk satin ribbon and on right-hand side with large applied rosette of twisted black silk satin ribbon, reaching the top of the crown and over.

Accession no. 1967.187.265

151. Hat, straw, about 1925-27

Hat of woven black straw, with deep, folded crown, lined with black silk. Brim turned up at centre back, the edge bound with black silk velvet. Crown decorated with black and dusty pink silk velvet ribbons, knotted at the centre front. Two large applied flowers in beige cotton velvet with yellow 'stamens' at centre front of crown. Labelled *Millinery Bon Marché (Liverpool) Ltd*
Accession no. 1967.187.287

152. Hat, woven fibre (?), about 1925-27

Hat of coffee-coloured woven fibre, the deep crown with indented top decorated with large cotton velvet flowers in pale grey, blue, lilac, brown and gold. Brim swept down at front and up at centre back, the edge bound with coffee-coloured silk petersham ribbon. Unlined.

Accession no. 1967.187.310

153. Hat, horsehair and silk crepe, about 1926-27

Hat of woven black horsehair, known as crin, the deep crown swathed with broad band of black silk crepe. Narrow brim of woven crin and silk crepe. Top of crown and brim decorated with stylised leaves embroidered in pale pink and brown silk chain stitch. Crown lined with black rayon silk.

Labelled *13/11* (price)

Accession no. 1967.187.312

154. Hat, straw, about 1910-20

Hat of woven natural straw, the rounded crown decorated with a swathe of dark navy blue silk satin and lined with cream-coloured silk. Wide brim decorated with applied purple cotton velvet pansies and leaves, lined with machine-made lace.

Labelled *K. & A. Lennon, Milliners and Costumiers, 349 Aigburth Road, Liverpool & 170 Poulton Road, Seacombe*

Accession no. 1967.187.322

155. Hat, straw, about 1918-20

Hat of woven natural straw, the deep, domed crown decorated with a garland of dried grasses and imitation wild flowers in red, yellow and green. Brim swept down at centre front and up at centre back. Unlined.

Accession no. 1967.187.303

156. Hat, straw, about 1920-24

Hat of woven natural straw, the deep, slightly pointed crown decorated with large embroidered flower and butterfly motifs in green, orange, purple and cream raffia. Elliptical brim, the slightly turned-up edge woven in an open pattern.

Accession no. 1967.187.263

157. Hat, straw, about 1920-24

Hat of woven dark navy blue straw, the deep, rounded crown with a moulded ridge to each side. Crown decorated with garland of blue cotton velvet flowers, with green foliage between them. Brim turned up at centre back. Unlined.

Accession no. 1967.187.254

158. Hat, straw, about 1920-24

Hat of woven natural straw, the tall beehive-shaped crown decorated with a deep band of dark brown cotton velvet and large bow at centre back. Edge of turned-up brim bound with dark brown cotton velvet. Unlined.

Accession no. WAG 2001.45.149

159. Hat, horsehair, about 1918-22

Hat of woven brown horsehair, known as crin, with a deep, slightly pointed crown and wide double-layered brim with wired edge. Decorated around the crown with a narrow ribbon of brown petersham and a garland of pink, purple, brown and blue cotton velvet flowers. Mother-of-pearl shell applied to some of the petals. Unlined.

Accession no. 1967.187.251

160. Hat, horsehair and silk net, about 1918-22

Hat of woven black horsehair, known as crin, the deep, domed crown covered with black silk net. Elliptical-shaped brim covered with black silk net and black machine-made lace. Decorated around the crown with a garland of pink and lilac silk roses and pale blue silk forget-me-nots. Lined with black silk.

Accession no. 1967.187.252

161. Hat, straw, about 1925-27

Hat of woven brown straw, with deep, domed crown and narrow brim, the edge bound with brown silk satin. Decorated around the crown with narrow band of brown silk petersham ribbon and with deep, ruffled flounce of brown machine-made lace. Lace flounce edged with three narrow bands of woven horsehair, known as crin. Brown celluloid brooch, set with diamanté pastes, at centre front of crown. Lined with brown rayon satin.

Accession no. 1967.187.291

162. Hat, straw, about 1924-26

Hat of finely woven blue straw, with rounded crown and elliptical-shaped brim with turned-up edge. Printed cotton scarf, in blue, black, orange and cream, swathed around crown and tied in knot at centre back. Lined with blue rayon silk.

Stamped *The Daelyne, Regd., British Make*

Accession no. 1967.187.301

163. Hat, straw, about 1922-24

Hat, woven mauve, green and yellow straw, the rounded crown with a moulded 'step' to the centre back. Wide brim, the edge bound with paisley-patterned printed cotton. Crown swathed with paisley-patterned printed cotton scarf in green and red.

Stamped *A Stuarson Hat* and labelled *Stuarson Hats, 378-33, AO, 121* and *No.dfl*

Accession no. 1967.187.281a

164. Cloche hat, straw, about 1925-28

Cloche hat of woven shiny green straw, with very deep crown and narrow brim, bound with green silk georgette. Decorated around the crown with deep, swathed band of gold silk satin, folded into bow-like shapes at each side of brim. Lined with pale grey rayon silk.

Stamped *A Payzway Hat* and labelled *Cripps, Sons & Co, 12, 14 & 16 Bold Street, Liverpool*

Accession no. 1967.187.278

165. Hat, straw and cotton velvet, about 1926-28

Hat of finely woven brown straw, with deep, domed crown and narrow brim, folded at centre front and turned up at centre back, the edge bound with cotton velvet. Crown decorated with two large applied leaf-shapes of brown cotton velvet, folded and overlapping, each scored with intersecting lines. Lined with beige-coloured rayon silk.

Stamped *A Mortimer Hat* and labelled *Cripps, Sons & Co., 12, 14 & 16 Bold Street, Liverpool*

Accession no. 1967.187.277

166. Hat, straw, about 1927-28

Hat of woven dark brown straw, with very deep, domed crown with 'pinched' effect at top, and down-swept brim, the edge bound with dark brown rayon satin. Crown decorated at centre front with deep, swathed and pleated band of dark brown rayon satin. Applied triangles of brown and cream silk braid and metallic gold rick rack braid at centre front. Lined with brown rayon silk.

Accession no. 1967.187.311

167. Cloche hat, straw, about 1928-30

Cloche hat of woven shiny black straw, with rounded crown, the brim turned back at centre front and down at both sides. No brim at centre back. Centre front decorated with applied 'swirl' shape, sewn with silver sequins and silver thread on a black silk satin ground. Crown decorated with deep, swathed band of black silk satin and with narrow, applied bands of silk sewn with silver sequins and silver thread. Lined with black rayon silk.

Accession no. 1967.187.271

168. Cloche hat, straw, about 1928-31

Cloche hat of finely woven pale green straw, the crown closely shaped to the head, the brim turned back flat at centre front. Front of crown inlaid with piece of green wool felt, the back bound with green wool felt. Gilt metal buckle attached to wool felt ribbon on right-hand side. Lined with pink-beige rayon silk.
Labelled *Cripps, Sons & Co., 12, 14 & 16 Bold Street, Liverpool*
Accession no. 1967.187.473

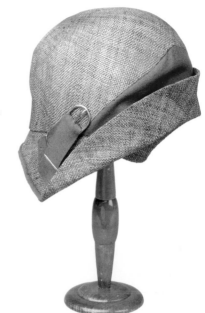

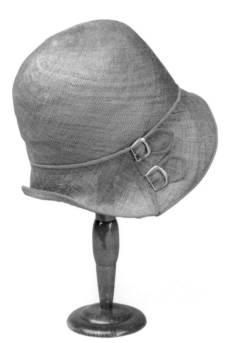

169. Cloche hat, straw, about 1928-31

Cloche hat of finely woven pale green straw, the crown closely shaped to the head, the brim turned down at centre front and sides and curled up at centre back. Bottom of crown and edge of brim both bound with paler green silk chiffon. Two decorative straps of straw edged with silk chiffon and set with gilt metal buckles at right-hand side of the brim. Lined with pale green rayon silk.
Stamped *A Craven Hat* and labelled *Cripps, Sons & Co., 12, 14 & 16 Bold Street, Liverpool*
Accession no. 1967.187.270

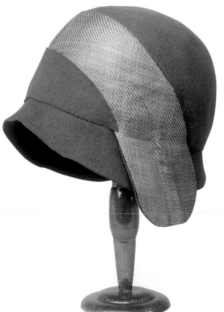

170. Cloche hat, wool felt and straw, about 1928-31

Cloche hat of chocolate-brown wool felt, the crown closely shaped to the head, the narrow brim turned slightly up at centre front and down at the sides and back. Middle section of crown, extending down over left side, of mid-brown woven straw. Lined with brown rayon silk.
Stamped *A Craven Hat, Rgd.,* and labelled *Cripps, Sons & Co., 12, 14 & 16 Bold Street, Liverpool*
Accession no. 1967.187.472

171. Cloche hat, wool felt and straw, about 1929-31

Cloche hat of dark brown wool felt, the closely fitted crown moulded and sewn all over into a diaper pattern and cut low down on the nape of the neck. Brim of finely woven brown straw folded and turned back flat on both sides of crown. Lined with dark brown rayon silk.
Labelled *Cripps, Sons & Co., 12, 14 & 16 Bold Street, Liverpool*
Accession no. 1967.187.269

172. Cloche hat, wool felt, about 1928-30

Cloche hat of chocolate brown wool felt, the deep, domed crown decorated at centre front with two large applied feathers on a cotton ground. Brim turned up at the back and pleated and turned up on the right-hand side. Lined with pink and blue shot silk.
Labelled *Cripps, Sons & Co., 12, 14 & 16 Bold Street, Liverpool*
Accession no. 1967.187.300

173. Hat, straw, about 1928-30

Hat of finely woven navy blue straw, the crown shaped closely to the head. The brim is edge bound with navy corded silk, folded back flat across crown at centre front and folded and swept down at each side. Deep, navy blue silk velvet ribbon around crown, with narrower ribbon threaded through centre front of brim. Lined with black rayon silk.
Stamped *De Moysey, 17 rue de L'Echiquier, Paris* and *Ranelagh Street, Liverpool*
Accession no. 1967.187.293

174. Hat, wool felt and straw, about 1930-32

Hat of dark brown wool felt, with deep, rounded crown and narrow brim. Crown has wide, integrated band of woven straw, striped pale green, yellow and brown. Large brown felt bow at centre back. Unlined except for narrow band of brown rayon silk.

Worn by one of the Tinne girls as a teenager.

Accession no. 1967.187.297

175. Hat, straw and wool, about 1930-32

Hat of woven yellow straw and wool, with rounded, folded crown and narrow brim. Decorated around crown with band of yellow petersham ribbon, twisted into small bow at centre back. Lined with yellow rayon silk.

Stamped *Reslaw Hat*

Worn by one of the Tinne girls as a teenager.

Accession no. 1967.187.302

176. Hat, straw, about 1930-32

Hat of finely woven pale grey straw, with rounded crown and gently sloping brim, the edge bound with pale grey corded silk. Crown decorated with band of grey silk petersham ribbon, formed into bow at centre back and held in place with half-ring of silvered metal. Lined with beige-coloured rayon silk.

Accession no. 1967.187.294

177. Hat, horsehair and straw, about 1930-32

Hat of woven dark brown horsehair, known as crin, with deep, rounded crown and narrow brim of woven shiny brown straw. Brim turned up at the left-hand side, on to the crown, and decorated with applied 'leaves' of brown cotton velvet.

Stamped *The Orb Make, Highest Grade*

Accession no. 1967.187.292

178. Hat, wool velour, about 1932-35

Hat of dark brown wool velour, the rounded crown gently pleated at centre front and back, narrow velour brim. Left side of crown decorated with two ruched and applied bands of red and yellow silk velvet, twisted together. Two bands of dark brown and orange striped petersham ribbon around crown and tied in small bow at centre back. Lined with dark brown rayon silk.

Embroidered *Reslaw Hat*

Accession no. 1967.187.308

179. Hat, straw, about 1932-35

Hat of woven shiny black straw, with low, rounded crown and wide brim. Crown decorated with band of black silk petersham ribbon and garland of cotton velvet flowers in shades of pink, blue and white. Lined with black rayon silk.

Accession no. 1967.187.276

180. Hat, straw, about 1932-35

Hat of woven shiny brown straw, with low, rounded crown and wide brim. Crown decorated with band of dark brown silk petersham ribbon, crossed over at centre front, and with large flower head and leaves in cream rayon silk and brown cotton velvet. Lined with dark brown rayon silk.

Stamped *"Yeltrow" Comfort Fitting Hat, Regd.*

Accession no. 1967.187.321

181. Hat, raffia, about 1932-35

Hat of woven beige-coloured raffia, with rounded crown and wide, floppy brim. Crown decorated with garland of artificial wild flowers, including buttercups, daisies and wild roses, in pink, yellow and green silk. Cream silk satin bows applied at centre front and back. Lined with cream rayon silk.

Accession no. 1967.187.304

182. Hat, straw, about 1932-35

Hat of woven shiny brown straw, the deep, rounded crown folded into a circular 'pleat' around the top and decorated with parallel lines of cream stitching down on to the brim. Narrow brim also decorated with triangular-shaped areas of parallel stitching. Crown decorated with rolled band of cream silk ribbon and brown straw, with bow at centre back. Lined with dark brown rayon silk.

Stamped *Paulette*

Accession no. 1967.187.320

183. Cocktail hat, horsehair, about 1932-35

Cocktail hat of woven black horsehair, known as crin, the crown a circular cap-shape, folded once on one side. Brim attached on one side, applied across top of crown and folded and pleated into shape on the other. Three orange-red plastic ball-shaped beads attached to one side of crown. Lined with black rayon silk.

Accession no. 1967.187.275

184. Hat, straw, about 1935-36

Hat of woven navy blue shiny straw, with low, rounded crown and wide brim, swept down at front and sides and up at centre back. Crown decorated with band of navy blue silk petersham ribbon and, in centre front, with applied broad petersham ribbon, pleated in contrasting navy blue and white folds. Lined with olive green rayon silk.

Labelled *Owen Owen Ltd, Liverpool, 12/9* (crossed out), *6/3* (reduced price)

Accession no. 1967.187.325

185. Hat, straw, about 1935-39

Boater-style hat of finely woven navy blue straw, with wide, shallow crown and wide brim. Brim of double-thickness straw with white silk petersham ribbon sandwiched between the layers. Crown decorated with pleated band of white silk petersham ribbon. Unlined, but band of navy blue silk velvet around inside of crown to secure hat to wearer's head.

Labelled *Modèles Luzy, Paris*

Accession no. 1967.187.319

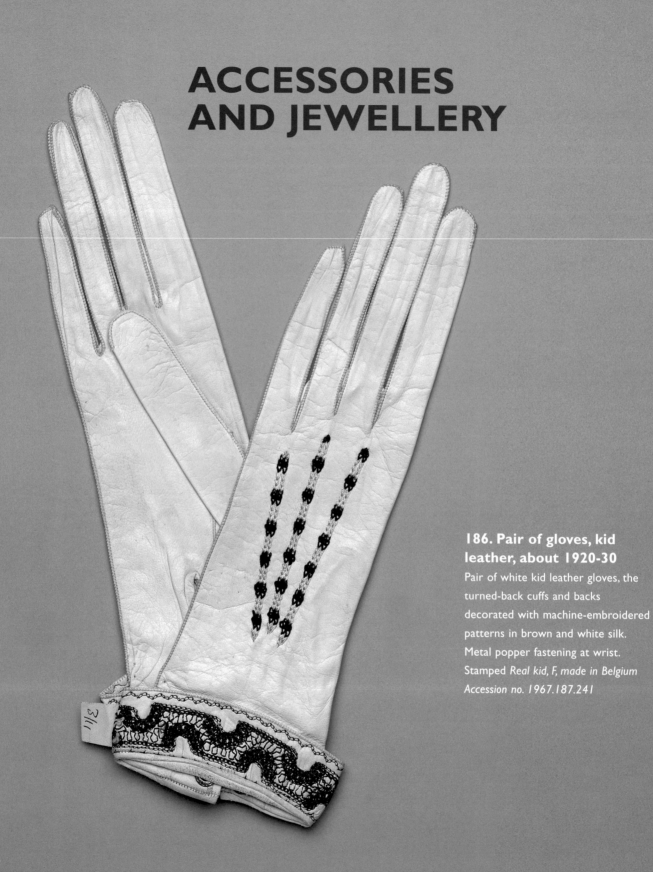

ACCESSORIES AND JEWELLERY

186. Pair of gloves, kid leather, about 1920-30
Pair of white kid leather gloves, the turned-back cuffs and backs decorated with machine-embroidered patterns in brown and white silk. Metal popper fastening at wrist. Stamped *Real kid, F, made in Belgium*
Accession no. 1967.187.241

187. Pair of gloves, kid leather, about 1920-30

Pair of dark brown kid leather gloves, the turned-back cuffs
and backs decorated with machine-embroidered patterns in
black and red silk. Metal popper fastening at wrist.
Stamped *Real kid, F, made in Belgium*
Accession no. 1967.187.238

188. Pair of gloves, kid leather, about 1920-30

Pair of white kid leather gloves, edged with
narrow band of black leather. Decorated on
backs with three lines of embroidered black
silk. Elasticated gusset let in at wrist.
Stamped *Real kid, made in Belgium* and
labelled *Lewis's Ltd, Price 3/11*
Accession no. 1967.187.242

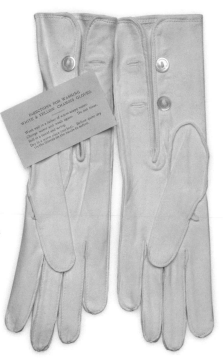

189. Pair of gloves, chamois leather, about 1928-35

Pair of white chamois leather gloves, completely plain, fastening with
two mother-of-pearl buttons at each wrist.
Original washing instructions printed on card inside one glove –
DIRECTIONS FOR WASHING WHITE & YELLOW CHAMOIS GLOVES. Wash
well in a lather of warm, soapy water. Change water and wash again. Do not
rinse. Roll in a towel and wring. Dry in a warm place (not hot). Before quite
dry, try the gloves on the hands to soften
Accession no. WAG 2001.45.135

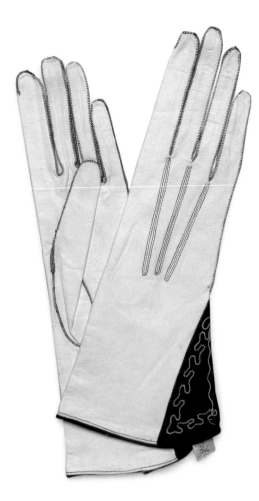

190. Pair of gloves, kid leather, about 1928-35

Pair of white kid leather gloves, gauntlet shape, with black leather gores set into the side seams, embroidered with white cotton stitching. Edge of gloves bound with black leather. Fingers and backs stitched with black cotton.

Stamped *Made in Italy* and labelled 2/- (crossed out) and 1/9
Accession no. 1967.187.244

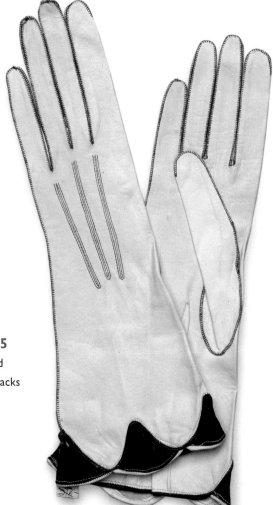

191. Pair of gloves, kid leather, about 1928-35

Pair of white kid leather gloves, gauntlet-shape, with scalloped black leather 'gores' set into the bottom edges. Fingers and backs stitched with black cotton. Elasticated gusset set in at wrist.
Labelled *2/11* (crossed out) and *2/9*
Accession no. 1967.187.245

192. Pair of gloves, knitted rayon, about 1930-34

Pair of cream-coloured knitted rayon silk gloves, gauntlet style, the edges of the scalloped, overlapping wrists piped with black and white rayon silk cord. Backs decorated with machine-embroidery in black and white rayon silk. Metal popper fastening at wrist.

Labelled *Artificial silk, Made in Germany* and *2/9*

Accession no. 1967.187.246

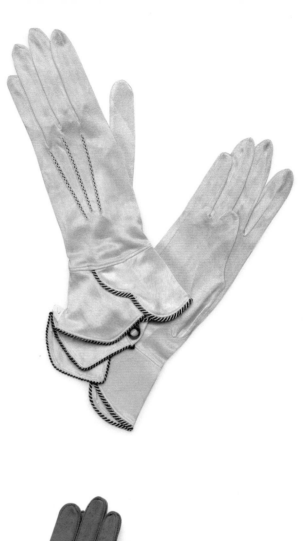

193. Pair of gloves, chamois leather, about 1930-35

Pair of white chamois leather gloves, gauntlet style, with contrasting black cotton running stitch around fingers. Backs decorated with three lines of black cotton running stitch.

Stamped *Washable* and *Leather gloves, Made in England*

Accession no. WAG 2001.45.131

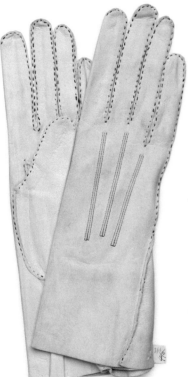

194. Pair of gloves, chamois leather, about 1928-35

Pair of beige-coloured chamois leather gloves, gauntlet style, with running stitch around fingers. Backs decorated with three lines of stitching. Elasticated wrists.

Stamped *English Make, Washable*

Accession no. WAG 2001.45.140

195. Pair of gloves, antelope suede, about 1930-35

Pair of tan-coloured antelope suede gloves, gauntlet style, with plaited suede edging to cuff and elasticated wrists. Backs decorated with three lines of stitching.
Stamped *Real Antelope, English Make, Washable* and labelled *LEWIS'S LTD, Price 10/6*
Accession no. WAG 2001.45.145

196. Pair of gloves, rayon silk, about 1930-35

Pair of dusty pink-coloured gloves of machine-knitted rayon silk, gauntlet style, with gores and piping to the edges of paler dusty pink-coloured rayon silk. Short strap and pearl bead button to each gore. Backs decorated with three lines of stitching.
Stamped *Artificial Silk, Made in England* and *Fournes Own Make*
Accession no. 1967.187.247

197. Pair of gloves, suede, about 1930-35

Pair of brown suede gloves, gauntlet style, the cuffs trimmed with dyed brown rabbit fur. Backs decorated with three lines of stitching. Lined with pale grey wool.
Stamped *7, English make*
Accession no. WAG 2001.45.129

198. Pair of evening gloves, cotton, about 1920-30

Pair of beige-coloured machine-knitted cotton evening gloves. Opening at wrist with three mother-of-pearl buttons. Backs decorated with three lines of silk stitching.
Accession no. 1967.187.248

199. Pair of evening gloves, cotton, about 1920-30

Pair of dark beige-coloured machine-knitted cotton evening gloves. Opening at wrist with two mother-of-pearl buttons and piped edging of white cotton. Backs decorated with three rows of stitching.
Accession no. 1967.187.249

200. Jabot, wool, 1912

Jabot of cream-coloured machine-knitted wool, with turtle-neckline and large ruffle to centre front panel. Fastens down centre back of neckline with three metal poppers.
In original box, marked The "DIANA" KNITTED JABOT, PAT. No 9653 OF 1912, and Made in Germany
Accession no. 1967.187.397

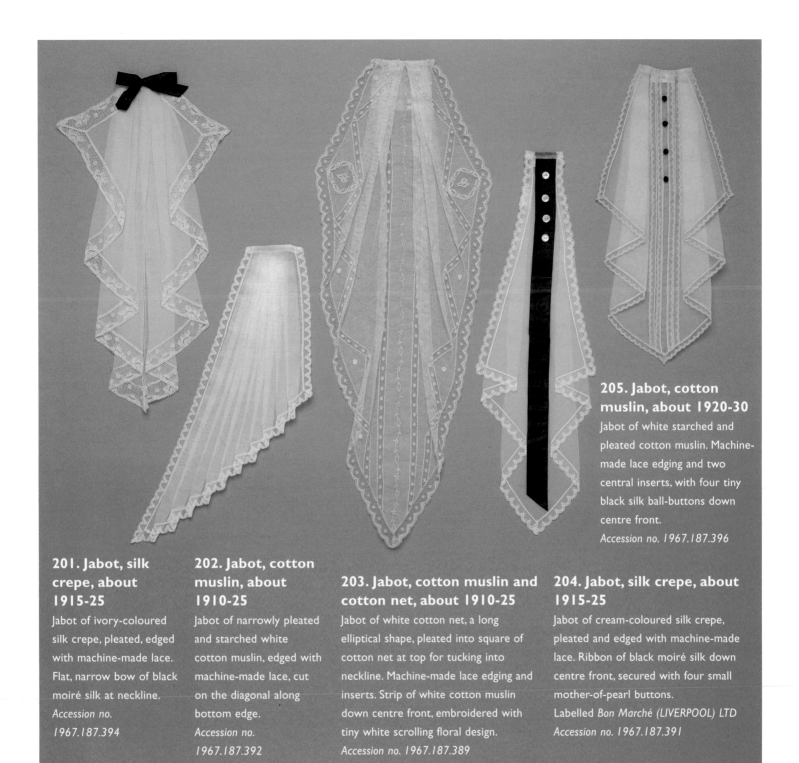

205. Jabot, cotton muslin, about 1920-30

Jabot of white starched and pleated cotton muslin. Machine-made lace edging and two central inserts, with four tiny black silk ball-buttons down centre front.

Accession no. 1967.187.396

201. Jabot, silk crepe, about 1915-25

Jabot of ivory-coloured silk crepe, pleated, edged with machine-made lace. Flat, narrow bow of black moiré silk at neckline.

Accession no. 1967.187.394

202. Jabot, cotton muslin, about 1910-25

Jabot of narrowly pleated and starched white cotton muslin, edged with machine-made lace, cut on the diagonal along bottom edge.

Accession no. 1967.187.392

203. Jabot, cotton muslin and cotton net, about 1910-25

Jabot of white cotton net, a long elliptical shape, pleated into square of cotton net at top for tucking into neckline. Machine-made lace edging and inserts. Strip of white cotton muslin down centre front, embroidered with tiny white scrolling floral design.

Accession no. 1967.187.389

204. Jabot, silk crepe, about 1915-25

Jabot of cream-coloured silk crepe, pleated and edged with machine-made lace. Ribbon of black moiré silk down centre front, secured with four small mother-of-pearl buttons.

Labelled *Bon Marché (LIVERPOOL) LTD*
Accession no. 1967.187.391

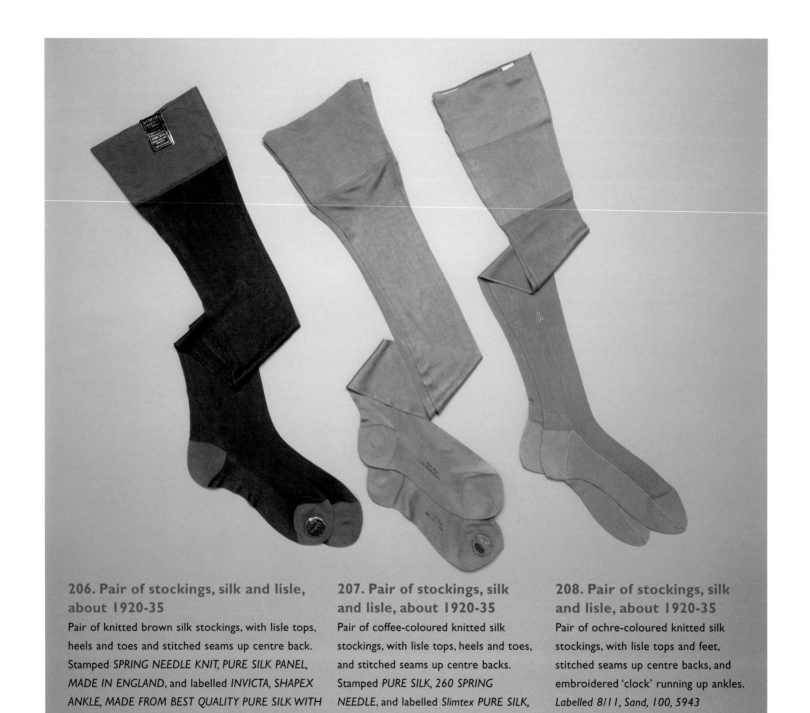

206. Pair of stockings, silk and lisle, about 1920-35

Pair of knitted brown silk stockings, with lisle tops, heels and toes and stitched seams up centre back. Stamped *SPRING NEEDLE KNIT, PURE SILK PANEL, MADE IN ENGLAND*, and labelled *INVICTA, SHAPEX ANKLE, MADE FROM BEST QUALITY PURE SILK WITH LISLE TOPS AND FEET, BRITISH MADE*, and *INVICTA, REGD., SHAPEX, BRITISH MADE*
Accession no. 1967.187.466

207. Pair of stockings, silk and lisle, about 1920-35

Pair of coffee-coloured knitted silk stockings, with lisle tops, heels and toes, and stitched seams up centre backs. Stamped *PURE SILK, 260 SPRING NEEDLE*, and labelled *Slimtex PURE SILK, SEAL OF SATISFACTION*
Accession no. 1967.187.464

208. Pair of stockings, silk and lisle, about 1920-35

Pair of ochre-coloured knitted silk stockings, with lisle tops and feet, stitched seams up centre backs, and embroidered 'clock' running up ankles.
Labelled 8/11, Sand, 100, 5943
Accession no. 1967.187.465

209. Headdress, egret feathers, about 1920-30
Headdress of dyed black egret feathers, the tips left white, wired together on circular frame, and secured at centre back with narrow elastic.
Accession no. 1967.187.474

210. Headddress, celluloid, about 1920-30

Headddress of black celluloid strips and sequins, mounted on stiff cotton tiara-shaped base, fastening at centre back with two long wire loops. Two rows of fanned-out celluloid strips, arranged one over the other, at centre front.

Accession no. 1967.187.475

211. Hair ornament, egret feathers, about 1920-30

Hair ornament of dyed black, curled egret feathers, secured at base with cotton thread.

Accession no. 1967.187.476

212. False hairpiece, human hair, about 1905-15
False hairpiece of auburn-coloured human hair, the circular, domed frame formed from wire and silk net. Edge bound with dark brown silk ribbon.
Accession no. 1967.187.338

213. False hairpiece, human hair, about 1905-15
False hairpiece of auburn-coloured human hair, a long oval shape, formed by woven horsehair beneath the human hair. In two layers, hollow in the centre.
Accession no. 1967.187.339

214. False hairpiece, human hair, about 1905-15
False hairpiece of auburn-coloured, wavy human hair, covered with fine, brown silk net. Domed, oval-shaped framework with hole at each end, the edge bound with green cotton tape.
Labelled *Good Goods Brand, Reg. no. 590 575, No......, Price, Gold Medallist* and *Highest Award, London, 1906*
Accession no. 1967.187.336

215. False hairpiece, human hair, about 1905-15
False hairpiece of auburn-coloured human hair, covered with fine black silk net. Domed, oval-shaped framework with hole at one end, the edge bound with brown silk ribbon.
Accession no. 1967.187.337

216. Necklace, pearlised plastic and diamanté pastes, about 1925-30
Necklace composed of alternating coiled silver wire and diamanté pastes, fastening with screw-threaded
fastener. Pendant composed of narrow strips of pale grey, pearlised plastic, fanned out into two 'wing'
shapes, each set into a diamanté paste mount and joined at centre front by a diamanté paste-covered bead.
Labelled *Bon Marché, Liverpool, Made in France, 35/-*
Accession no. *1967.187.426*

217. Necklace and pair of dress clips, pearlised plastic and gilt metal, about 1925-35

Necklace composed of six narrow, plaited gilt metal braids, held together at sides with gilt metal clips and fastening with screw-threaded fastener. Large daisy head-shaped pendant of narrow, pale blue pearlised plastic 'petals', with decorative gilt metal centre. Pair of matching dress clips of pearlised plastic 'petals' with decorative gilt metal centres.

Accession no. 1967.187.428a & b

218. Necklace and dress clip, pearlised plastic and gilt metal, about 1925-35

Necklace composed of six narrow, plaited gilt metal braids, held together at sides with gilt metal clips and fastening with screw-threaded fastener. Large daisy head-shaped pendant of narrow, pale pink pearlised plastic 'petals', with decorative gilt metal centre. Matching single dress clip of pearlised plastic 'petals' with decorative gilt metal centre.

Accession no. 1967.187.427a & b

220. Hatpin, steel, base metal and glass pastes, about 1900-10

Steel hatpin, the silvered base metal head worked in the form of a decorative filigree dome set with pale blue glass pastes.

Accession no. 1967.187.436

221. Four hatpins, steel and glass, about 1900-20

Four steel hatpins, two of them longer than the others, all with black glass bead-shaped heads.

Accession no. 1967.187.440

219. Pair of hatpins, steel, silver and enamel, 1909

Pair of steel hatpins, the silver button-shaped tops of amber-coloured enamel over an engine-turned ground.

Birmingham assay mark for 1909

Inscribed *B.J.D. April 2nd 1910*

Accession no. 1967.187.433

222. Hatpin, steel and silver, 1917

Steel hatpin, the silver head in the form of an open flower, the petals slightly curled over.

Birmingham assay mark for 1917

Maker's mark *P & T*

Accession no. 1967.187. 434

223. Pair of hatpins, steel and silver, about 1900-10

Pair of steel hatpins, with small heads of silver filigree and wirework, worked in a stylised floral shape and set with silver beads.

Accession no. 1967.187.437

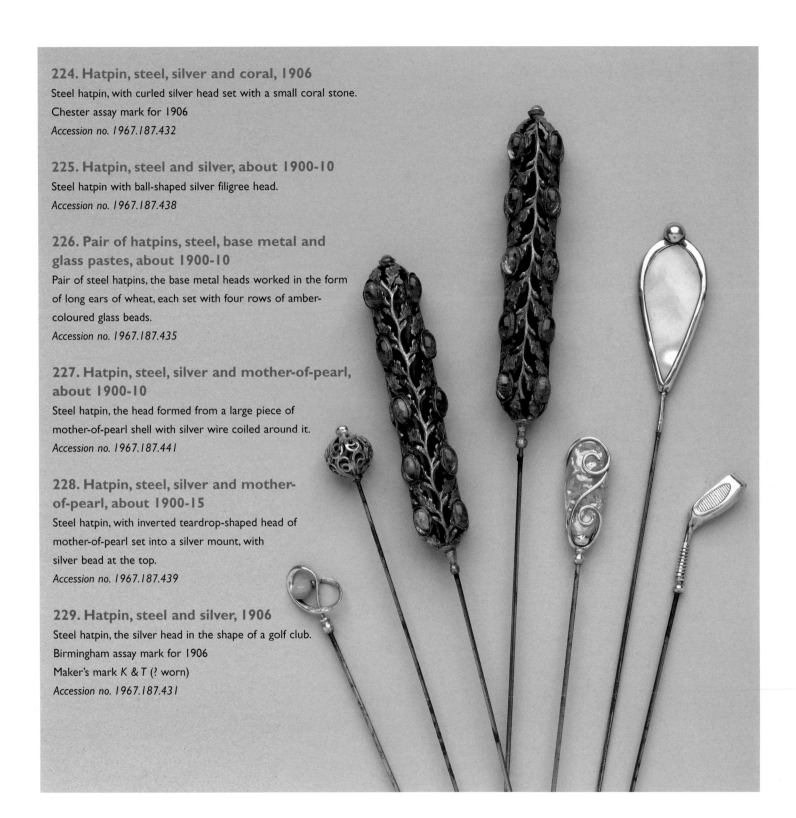

224. Hatpin, steel, silver and coral, 1906
Steel hatpin, with curled silver head set with a small coral stone.
Chester assay mark for 1906
Accession no. 1967.187.432

225. Hatpin, steel and silver, about 1900-10
Steel hatpin with ball-shaped silver filigree head.
Accession no. 1967.187.438

226. Pair of hatpins, steel, base metal and glass pastes, about 1900-10
Pair of steel hatpins, the base metal heads worked in the form of long ears of wheat, each set with four rows of amber-coloured glass beads.
Accession no. 1967.187.435

227. Hatpin, steel, silver and mother-of-pearl, about 1900-10
Steel hatpin, the head formed from a large piece of mother-of-pearl shell with silver wire coiled around it.
Accession no. 1967.187.441

228. Hatpin, steel, silver and mother-of-pearl, about 1900-15
Steel hatpin, with inverted teardrop-shaped head of mother-of-pearl set into a silver mount, with silver bead at the top.
Accession no. 1967.187.439

229. Hatpin, steel and silver, 1906
Steel hatpin, the silver head in the shape of a golf club.
Birmingham assay mark for 1906
Maker's mark *K & T* (? worn)
Accession no. 1967.187.431

BABIES' AND CHILDREN'S CLOTHES

Left to right: Bertha Tinne, housemaid
Elizabeth, Helen Tinne, outside Clayton
Lodge, about 1924.

230. Baby's binder, cotton and wool flannel, about 1911-20s

Baby's white cotton binder, rectangular with five narrow cotton tapes sewn on at each end for securing it to the body. Separate, rectangular length of cream-coloured wool flannel, worn inside the binder for extra warmth.

Accession no. WAG 2001.45.114

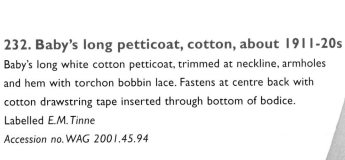

231. Baby's vest, cotton lawn, about 1911-20s

Baby's white cotton lawn vest, trimmed at neckline and armholes with machine-made lace. Fastens at centre back of neckline with narrow cotton tape ties.

Accession no. WAG 2001.45.102

232. Baby's long petticoat, cotton, about 1911-20s

Baby's long white cotton petticoat, trimmed at neckline, armholes and hem with torchon bobbin lace. Fastens at centre back with cotton drawstring tape inserted through bottom of bodice.

Labelled *E.M. Tinne*

Accession no. WAG 2001.45.94

233. Baby's long petticoat, brushed cotton, about 1911-20s

Baby's long cream-coloured brushed cotton petticoat, fastening at centre back with wrap-over flaps and tapes. Neckline, armholes and scallop-edged hem all embroidered with cream-coloured silk.

Accession no. WAG 2001.45.96

234. Baby's short petticoat, cotton, about 1913-20s

Baby's short white cotton petticoat, fastening down centre back with row of tiny buttons. Neckline, armholes and hem all scallop-edged and embroidered with white silk. Bottom of skirt decorated with pin-tucks and whitework embroidery.

Accession no. WAG 2001.45.98

235. Toddler's short petticoat, cotton, about 1925

Toddler's short white cotton petticoat, the wide neckline and armholes scallop-edged and threaded with a cotton tape drawstring. Centre front of bodice decorated with V-shaped section of drawn threadwork. Band of drawn threadwork at hem, with dagged and embroidered edge. May have belonged to Alexine Tinne (1923-2011).
Accession no. WAG 2001.45.99

236. Young child's drawers, cotton, about 1913-20s

Pair of young child's white cotton drawers, fastening at either side of waistband with a button, both now missing. Narrow band of drawn threadwork at each knee, and cotton ruffle trimmed with torchon bobbin lace.
Labelled *Sterling, £, Lock Stitch, Trade Mark, S & S*
Made by Stapley and Smith of London Wall
Accession no. 1967.187.176

237. Young girl's bodice, cotton twill, about 1915-20s

Young girl's cream-coloured cotton twill bodice, lacing up centre back with long cotton lace and fastening down centre front with row of eight bone buttons. Boned down the back. Separate side sections with elasticated cotton suspenders attached, the metal fasteners now missing. All edges bound with cream-coloured cotton tape.
Labelled *The S & S Comforto Bodice*
Made by Stapley and Smith of London Wall
Accession no. 1967.187.179

238. Young child's combinations, wool, about 1918-20s

Young child's cream-coloured machine-knitted woollen combinations, fastening down centre front with row of four buttons, two of them linen-covered, one mother-of-pearl and one plastic. Opening between legs. Cuffs at wrists and ankles.

Labelled *Reform, C.B., Guaranteed Quality,* with sheep's head logo

Made by Charles Bayer of London Wall.

Accession no. 1967.187.469

239. Young girl's nightdress, cotton, about 1916-17

Young girl's white cotton nightdress, the front placket fastening with three linen-covered buttons. Turned-over collar and turned-back cuffs both trimmed with ruffles of broderie anglaise.

Inscribed in ink *E.D. Tinne,* for Elspeth Deborah Tinne (1911-2000).

Accession no. 1967.187.172

240. Baby's christening gown, cotton lawn, about 1911

Baby's long christening gown of white cotton lawn, fastening at centre back of bodice with narrow cotton tape ties. Bodice, sleeves and skirt all decorated with floral whitework embroidery, swags and bows and cutwork butterflies. Scallop-edged broderie anglaise hem. White silk ribbon threaded through slots in cuffs and at bottom edge of bodice.

Worn by most of the Tinne children for their christenings at St Anne's Church, Aigburth, Liverpool, 1911-29.

Accession no. WAG 2001.45.88

241. Baby's long gown, cotton, about 1911-20s

Baby's long white cotton gown, fastening at centre back of bodice with narrow cotton tape tie. Ruched bodice front and centre front panel of skirt both decorated with alternating pin-tucks and inserted bands of broderie anglaise edged with whitework embroidery in featherstitch. Armholes and edges of skirt panel trimmed with broderie anglaise ruffle.

Labelled *E.M. Tinne*

Accession no. WAG 2001.45.91

242. Baby's long gown, cotton lawn, about 1911-20s

Baby's long white cotton lawn gown, with long sleeves, fastening at centre back of bodice with narrow cotton tape tie. Bodice decorated with alternating pintucks and inserted bands of whitework-embroidered braid. Skirt decorated in lower section with alternating horizontal pin-tucks and inserted bands of machine-made Bedfordshire lace. Crocheted trimming to hem.

Accession no. WAG 2001.45.92

243. Baby's short dress, cotton lawn, about 1911-20s

Baby's short white cotton lawn dress, fastening at centre back of bodice with cotton drawstring through waistband. Sleeve edgings, bodice front, inverted V-shaped panel to centre front of skirt and hemline all of broderie anglaise.

Accession no. 1967.187.132

244. Baby's short dress, cotton lawn, about 1916-17s

Baby's short white cotton lawn dress, with long sleeves, fastening at centre back of bodice with row of buttons. Bodice and hem decorated with pin-tucks, bands of broderie anglaise and machine-made lace insertions. Narrow band of pale green silk ribbon threaded through bottom of bodice, finishing in ribbon rosette with long pendant streamers on left-hand side.

Accession no. WAG 2001.45.77

245. Baby's short dress, cotton lawn, about 1911-20s

Baby's short white cotton lawn dress, with long sleeves, fastening at centre back of bodice with row of tiny buttons. High-necked bodice composed of alternating strips of whitework-embroidered braid and machine-made Valenciennes lace insertions. Cuffs, skirt front and hem all decorated with inserted or applied bands of machine-made Valenciennes lace.

Accession no. 1967.187.136

246. Baby's short dress, silk crepe de chine, about 1920-30

Baby's short white silk crepe de chine dress, with short puffed sleeves, fastening down centre back of bodice with row of tiny buttons. Narrow bodice decorated with vertical pin-tucks and machine-made Valenciennes lace insertions. Pin-tucks and trimming of machine-made Valenciennes lace at hem.
Accession no. WAG 2001.45.86

247. Baby's short dress, silk crepe, about 1920-30

Baby's short white silk crepe dress, with short puffed sleeves, fastening at centre back of bodice with row of buttons. Covered with layer of machine-embroidered net, the embroidery concentrated on the bodice and at the scallop-edged hem.
Accession no. WAG 2001.45.87

248. Baby's blouse, cotton lawn, about 1920-30

Baby's white cotton lawn blouse, with long sleeves, fastening at neckline with single tiny mother-of-pearl button. Turned-over collar, turned-back cuffs and front edges of blouse all decorated with floral cutwork embroidery.
Accession no. WAG 2001.45.100

249. Baby's cardigan, wool, about 1911-20s

Baby's cream hand-knitted woollen cardigan, double-breasted
but no fastenings, long sleeves.

Accession no. WAG 2001.45.101

250. Toddler's dress, cotton lawn, about 1913-20

Toddler's short white cotton lawn dress, with long sleeves,
fastening down centre back with row of buttons. Turned-over
collar and cuffs both trimmed with torchon bobbin lace and
whitework-embroidered braid insertions. Vertical tucks and
broderie anglaise panels to centre front of bodice. Horizontal
tucks to skirt and broderie anglaise scallop-edged hemline.

Accession no. 1967.187.130

251. Toddler's dress, cotton, about 1914

Toddler's short white cotton dress, with long plain sleeves and plain, full
skirt gathered into waistline. Fastens down centre back with row of
buttons. Peter Pan collar, bodice front and waistline all embroidered
with scrolling design in royal blue cotton.

Elspeth Tinne, born in May 1911, is pictured opposite wearing this dress,
aged about three, in a family photograph. She poses with her brother,
John Ernest Tinne, born in November 1913.

Accession no. 1967.187.134

John Ernest and Elspeth Deborah Tinne aged about three, about 1914.

252. Young girl's dress, rayon silk, about 1920-30

Young girl's short ivory-coloured rayon silk dress, with long sleeves, fastening down centre back with row of buttons. Bodice front and sleeves above the cuffs both hand-smocked. Turned-over collar and turned-back cuffs both embroidered with zig-zag pattern and French knots in cream-coloured silk. Cream silk zig-zag line embroidered above hem.

Accession no. 1967.187.131

253. Toddler's dress, cotton muslin, about 1926

Toddler's short white cotton muslin dress, with short sleeves and plain round neckline with V-shaped opening at centre front. Two patch pockets, the low waistline marked by muslin band threaded through pocket tops and tying at centre back. Crocheted edge to sleeves and two deep bands of crochet at hem.

Labelled 6

Probably worn by Alexine Tinne (1923-2011) aged about three

Accession no. WAG 2001.45.76

254. Young girl's dress, cotton lawn, about 1915-16
Young girl's white cotton lawn dress, with long sleeves, fastening down centre back with row of buttons. Pin-tucked bodice front and low waistline. Sleeves, bodice and skirt all decorated with alternating bands of whitework embroidery and machine lace insertions.
Worn by Elspeth Tinne (1911-2000), aged four to five years
Accession no. WAG 2001.45.75

255. Young girl's dress, cotton organdie, about 1917-18
Young girl's pale blue cotton organdie party dress, with elbow-length sleeves, fastening down centre back with row of buttons. Round neckline decorated with three organdie ruffles, the cuffs trimmed with two ruffles. Skirt decorated with three rows of ruffles above and at the hem. Waistline marked by ribbon of dusty pink velvet, with velvet bow at either side of centre front.
Accession no. 1967.187.127

256. Young girl's dress, cotton lawn, about 1920-25

Young girl's white cotton lawn party dress, with elbow-length sleeves, fastening down centre back with row of buttons. Rounded neckline decorated with double-frilled collar of needlerun net. Double frill of cotton lawn down outer seam of sleeves, and four vertical frills to centre front of bodice. Low waistline, bound with narrow black velvet ribbon and velvet bow on left hip. Flounced skirt with seven rows of frills. All frills hand-embroidered in orange, blue, black and yellow silk.

Accession no. 1967.187.126

257. Young girl's dress, tussah silk, about 1918-19

Young girl's natural-coloured tussah silk dress, with long sleeves, fastening down centre back with row of buttons. Yoke and cuffs both smocked and embroidered with brown silk. Deep, turned-over collar also embroidered with brown silk border and motifs.

Probably worn by Elspeth Tinne (1911-2000) aged seven to eight.

Accession no. 1967.187.149

258. Young girl's smock dress, cotton denim, about 1921-23

Young girl's pale blue cotton denim smock dress, with long plain sleeves, fastening down centre back with row of buttons. Plain bodice, the seams decorated with white woollen running stitch, the deep turned-over collar embroidered with floral motif in white wool. Plain skirt, the hem let down at some point to extend wear. Embroidered *TINNE* on inside of neckline in green silk.

Accession no. 1967.187.146

Bertha Emily, Elspeth Deborah and John Ernest Tinne, about 1918-19. Elspeth wears a natural-coloured tussah silk dress, Cat. no. 260.

Elspeth, Ernest, Bertha, Helen, and Alexine Tinne, about 1926. Bertha wears the tussah silk dress, Cat. no. 260, passed down to her by her older sister, Elspeth.

259. Young girl's dress, wool, about 1923-25

Young girl's brown hand-knitted woollen dress, with short sleeves and square-cut neckline. Bands of crocheted wool to neckline, sleeves and scallop-edged hem. Knitted drawstring cord through waistline, ending in two woollen pom-poms. Very similar to a dress worn by Bertha Tinne (1916-75), aged about eight, 1924. See page 146.

Accession no. WAG. 2003.11.5

260. Young girl's dress, tussah silk, about 1918-19

Young girl's natural-coloured tussah silk dress, with long sleeves, fastening down centre back with row of buttons. Bodice front and cuffs both smocked and embroidered with brown silk. Deep turned-over collar also embroidered with circular motifs in brown silk chain stitch. Two horizontal tucks to skirt above hemline.
Worn by Elspeth Tinne (1911-2000) aged about seven to eight, and then by Bertha Tinne (1916-75), aged about ten, 1926 in family photographs, pages 159-160.

Accession no. 1967.187.148

261. Young girl's dress, wool gabardine, about 1921-24

Young girl's navy blue wool gabardine dress, with long plain sleeves and turned-back cuffs. Two pleats to hips, low pockets, their top edges bound with black silk braid. Linen turned-over collar with hand-embroidered design in blue and yellow silk on silk gauze petal shapes. Row of wool-covered buttons down centre front of bodice. Half-belt at back at hip level. Half-lining of white cotton twill.
Probably worn by Elspeth Tinne (1911-2000).
Accession no. 1967.187.125

262. Young girl's dress, cotton organdie, about 1924-26

Young girl's white cotton organdie dress with short sleeves. Sleeve edgings, turned-down collar, vertical bands down either side of bodice front and the low waistband all made of mid-blue cotton organdie. Plain skirt, gathered into soft pleats over hips. Centre front of bodice decorated with rectangular grid of drawn threadwork embroidery with dots of blue silk.
Probably worn by Elspeth Tinne (1911-2000).
Labelled *14*
Accession no. 1967.187.143

263. Young girl's middy blouse and skirt, wool serge, about 1916-17

Young girl's navy blue wool serge middy blouse and matching skirt. Front-fastening blouse with fly-front concealing the buttons, plain sailor's collar, patch pocket on left breast and long sleeves with plain, flat-pleated cuffs. Elasticated bottom edge. Crowned crossed anchor motif and three stripes embroidered in gold silk thread on upper left sleeve.
Full skirt, pleated into waistband and fastening with button at centre back. Five narrow bands of navy blue wool braid applied above hemline.
Blouse labelled *Hope Brothers Ltd, 44-46 Ludgate Hill, London E.C.*
Probably worn by Elspeth Tinne (1911-2000) aged about five to six.
Accession nos. 1967.187.169 & 168b

264. Young boy's sailor jacket, cotton drill, about 1918

Young boy's white cotton drill sailor jacket, with long plain sleeves and plain white sailor collar. Front-fastening with linen-covered buttons concealed by fly-front, and with two linen tape ties. Patch pocket on left breast. Shown here with detachable sailor collar and cuffs of navy blue and white striped cotton.

Jacket labelled *G.H. Lee & Co. Ltd, Basnett Street, Liverpool*

Probably worn by John Ernest Tinne (1913-96)

Accession nos. 1967.187.166, 1967.187.184d (collar) and *1967.187.185h & i* (cuffs)

265. Young boy's sailor suit, cotton, about 1918-20

Young boy's blue and white striped cotton sailor suit. Jacket with long sleeves, sailor collar and drawstring through bottom edge. Fastens down centre front with linen-covered buttons concealed by fly-front. Patch pocket on left breast. Two white linen tape ties at centre front of neckline. Pair of matching shorts, with fly-front fastening and two side pockets.

Jacket labelled *G.H. Lee & Co. Ltd, Basnett Street, Liverpool*

Probably worn by John Ernest Tinne (1913-96)

Accession no. 1967.187.167a & b

266. Young child's bathing costume, cotton jersey, about 1920-30

Young child's navy blue machine-knitted cotton jersey bathing costume. Fastens on left shoulder with two buttons. Bands of red and white striped cotton jersey at neckline, armholes and legholes.

Accession no. 1967.187.470

267. Baby's coat, corded silk, about 1911-20s

Baby's coat of cream corded silk, lined with cream Jap silk, fastening at neck with two silk satin ribbon ties. Turned-over collar and long sleeves with turned-back cuffs. Bottom edge of coat and edges of collar and cuffs all scalloped and embroidered with floral motifs in cream silk.

Accession no. 1967.187.160

268. Baby's coat, silk, about 1911-12

Baby's cream silk coat, double-breasted, the buttons now missing, with wide pleats to centre front. Turned-over collar with deep flounce of cream silk broderie anglaise and floral embroidery in cream silk. Long sleeves with turned-back cuffs, also with floral embroidery in cream silk. Unlined. Worn by Elspeth Tinne (1911-2000).

Accession no. WAG 2001.45.71

164

269. Baby's coat, cotton poplin, about 1915-20s

Baby's white cotton poplin coat, fastening down centre front with two small mother-of-pearl buttons. Deep, square-cut turned-over collar with machine-made whitework inserts and frill of broderie anglaise. Long sleeves with broderie anglaise-trimmed cuffs. Bottom edge decorated with whitework inserts and broderie anglaise frill. Unlined.

Accession no. 1967.187.159

270. Toddler's coat, wool cashmere, about 1913-14

Toddler's cream wool cashmere coat, lined with white cotton sateen, fastening down centre front with four decorative mother-of-pearl buttons. Box pleats to centre front. Deep, turned-over collar, partly backed with cream silk and decorated with broderie anglaise inserts and frill. Long sleeves with broderie anglaise applied at cuffs.

Labelled *6271* in tiny punched holes

Worn by Elspeth Tinne (1911-2000) aged about two to three, in family photograph opposite.

Accession no. 1967.187.154

271. Toddler's coat, cotton muslin, about 1913-20s

Toddler's white sprigged cotton muslin coat, fastening down centre front with six mother-of-pearl buttons. Gathered into yoke at front and back. Deep, turned-over collar and turned-back cuffs to long sleeves both decorated with whitework insertions and broderie anglaise flounce at edges. Unlined.

Accession no. 1967.187.158

Elspeth Tinne, (1911-2000) aged two to three, about 1913-14, Cat. no. 270.

272. Toddler's coat, wool cashmere, about 1915-20s

Toddler's cream wool cashmere coat, lined with white cotton sateen, fastening down centre front with five mother-of-pearl buttons. Turned-over collar and turned-back cuffs to the long sleeves both bound at the edges with cream silk braid and embroidered with scrolling leaf design in cream silk.

Accession no. 1967.187.156

273. Toddler's coat, wool, about 1915-20s

Toddler's cream wool coat, lined with white cotton, double-breasted, fastening with six large mother-of-pearl buttons. Plain, turned-over collar and turned-back cuffs to the long sleeves. Small patch pocket in lower left side of lining.

Accession no. 1967.187.152

274. Toddler's coat, cotton poplin, about 1915-20s

Toddler's white cotton poplin coat, double-breasted, fastening with six large mother-of-pearl buttons. Turned-over collar and turned-back cuffs to the long sleeves both scallop-edged and decorated with floral whitework embroidery. Half belt at centre back. Unlined.

Accession no. 1967.187.157a

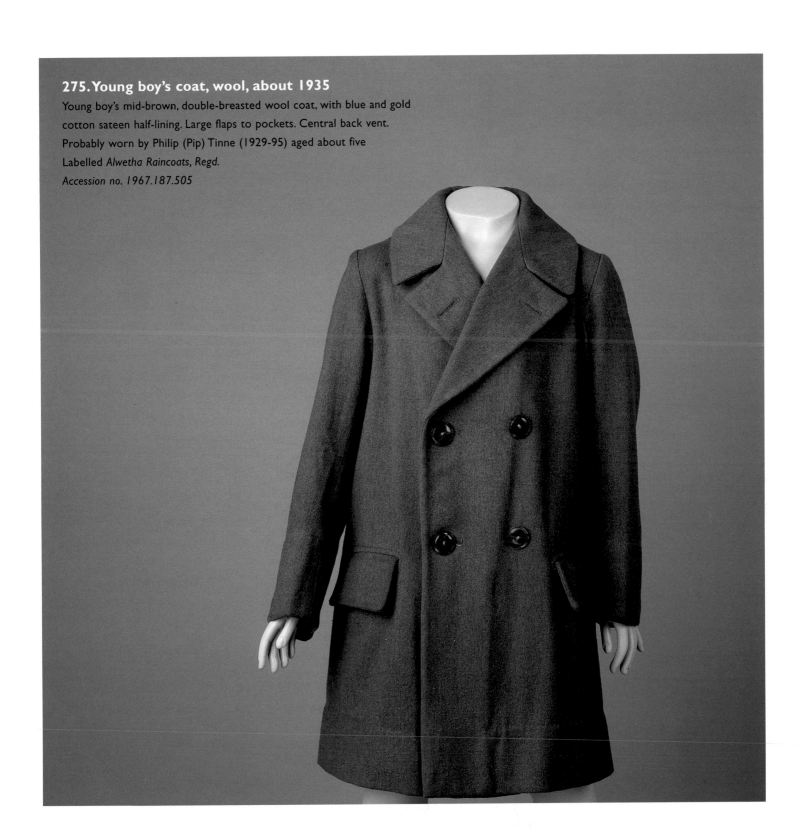

275. Young boy's coat, wool, about 1935

Young boy's mid-brown, double-breasted wool coat, with blue and gold cotton sateen half-lining. Large flaps to pockets. Central back vent.

Probably worn by Philip (Pip) Tinne (1929-95) aged about five

Labelled *Alwetha Raincoats, Regd.*

Accession no. 1967.187.505

276. Baby's collar, cotton muslin, about 1911-20s

Baby's white cotton muslin collar, the inner section supported on a slightly padded cotton under-collar and embroidered with floral whitework design. Outer section decorated with machine-made Valenciennes lace insert and edging. Fastens at centre back with tiny mother-of-pearl button and loop.
Labelled *E.M. TINNE*
Accession no. 1967.187.186a

277. Baby's collar, cotton piqué, about 1911-20s

Baby's white cotton piqué collar, supported by under-collar of white cotton twill. Decorative, embroidered edge, and embroidered all over with white dots in circles and triangles. Fastens at centre back with cotton-covered button and loop. *Accession no. 1967.187.186c*

278. Baby's collar, cotton muslin, about 1911-20s

Baby's white cotton muslin collar, supported by slightly padded cotton under-collar. Decorated with floral whitework embroidery. Scalloped edge. Fastens at centre back with cotton-covered button and loop.
Accession no. 1967.187.186b

279. Baby's collar, cotton muslin, about 1911-20s

Baby's white cotton muslin collar, supported by slightly padded cotton under-collar. Embroidered all over with floral whitework motifs. Decorative, embroidered edge, with piece of muslin attached horizontally at the bottom. Row of slots, meant to take coloured silk ribbon.
Labelled *Owen Owen Ltd, Liverpool, 1/6?*
Accession no. 1967.187.186

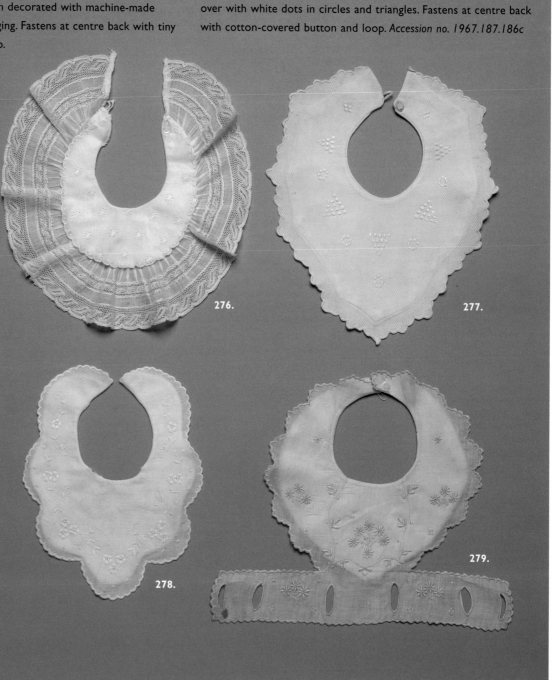

276.

277.

278.

279.

280. Pair of girl's stockings, wool, about 1935-45

Pair of girl's black, knee-length machine-knitted woollen stockings. Stamped *Spliced knee, ankle, heel & foot*, on the foot, and labelled *W.H. Watts & Co Ltd, Liverpool*, and *4/1 Ribs, Diamond knees, perfect fitting, all wearing parts are extra spliced, fast dye, special finish*
Accession no. 1967.187.193

281. Pair of girl's stockings, wool, about 1941-45

Pair of girl's black, knee-length machine-knitted woollen stockings.
Stamped *2 Fold Botany wool, 3 Fold ankle & foot, for school and gym wear, Made in England, Size 8*, and with Utility mark, *CC41, k 7/2 1592*
Accession no. 1967.187.191

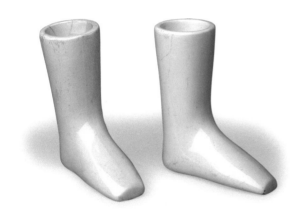

282. Pair of child's sock-dryers, glazed earthenware, about 1907-24

Pair of child's white glazed earthenware sock-dryers in the form of two hollow feet up to ankle level. Damp socks were drawn over them to dry out.
Stamped *Wedgwood, 3CO*, the factory's date-code for 1907-24
Accession no. 1967.187.203

283. Pair of child's shoes, cotton canvas, about 1915-30s

Pair of child's white cotton canvas shoes, fastening with two small white boot-buttons on the vamps. Leather soles and low stacked leather heels.
Stamped *Bally's, Swiss Manufacture*
In original shoebox, labelled *Button shoes, white, Bally, Manufactured in Switzerland*
Accession no. 1967.187.200

INVENTORY OF THE TINNE COLLECTION

All items in the Collection are listed here in museum accession number-order, and in the order in which they were acquired, in 1967, 2001 and 2003. They are grouped together by type of garment, for ease of reference, and entries with accession numbers highlighted in bold are those which are included and illustrated in the Selective Catalogue.

I. DAY CLOTHES

1967.187.7 Day dress, pale blue wool, black velvet trimmings, about 1912-14. Cat. no. 4.

1967.187.8 Day dress, pale grey wool, applied embroidery and grey silk braid, about 1912. Cat. no. 5.

1967.187.9 Summer day dress, woven silk net over white cotton sateen, labelled *Henry Darling & Co., Edinburgh*, about 1910-12.

1967.187.10 Summer day dress, blue, green and white striped cotton voile, about 1910. Cat. no. 2.

1967.187.11 Summer day dress, cream-coloured figured cotton voile and silk taffeta lining, about 1910.

1967.187.12 Summer day dress, white cotton lawn, whitework embroidery, about 1910-12. Cat. no. 3.

1967.187.14 Day dress, blue cotton velvet, fox fur trimming, the fabric stamped *Worrall's Fast Dye*, about 1914-16. Cat. no. 6.

1967.187.15 Day dress, navy blue cotton velvet, applied cut steel beads, about 1914-16.

1967.187.17 Summer day dress, white cotton muslin, cutwork and whitework embroidery, about 1916-18.

1967.187.18 Summer day dress, natural-coloured tussah silk, floral hand-embroidery, about 1916-18. Cat. no. 9.

1967.187.19 Maternity dress, black tussah silk, three-quarter length over-tunic, about 1920-25. Other maternity clothes survive in the collection. See Cat. nos. I and 114.

1967.187.21 Day dress, brown, white and orange printed silk and rayon, machine-made lace collar and cuffs, about 1924-25. Cat. no. 11. With matching coat, 1967.187.20. See entry below, in Outdoor Clothes and Furs.

1967.187.22 Afternoon dress, aubergine-coloured silk satin and silk damask, about 1925-27. Cat. no. 15.

1967.186.23 Afternoon dress, mid-blue silk velvet devoré and coffee-coloured silk, about 1925-27.

1967.187.24 Afternoon dress, black wool crepe, applied circles of red wool crepe, large red plastic buckle to centre front, about 1925. Cat. no. 12.

1967.187.25 Afternoon dress, terracotta brown silk crepe, fringed over-skirt, about 1925. Cat. no. 13.

1967.187.26 Afternoon dress, dusty pink rayon grosgrain, rosette on left shoulder, about 1926-27.

1967.187.27 Afternoon dress, pinky-brown silk crepe, machine embroidery, about 1925-27.

1967.187.28 Under-slip, coffee-coloured Jap silk, with broad shoulder straps, worn beneath 1967.187.27, about 1925-27.

1967.187.29 Summer day dress, black silk chiffon, printed floral pattern in pale blue, cream and brown, about 1929-32. Cat. no. 17.

1967.187.30 Afternoon dress, dark brown rayon crepe, salmon-pink silk crepe trimmings, about 1925-27.

1967.187.31 Afternoon dress, chocolate brown silk crepe, panels of machine embroidery, about 1925-27.

1967.187.33 Afternoon dress, black ribbed rayon, white silk crepe trimmings, about 1925-28.

1967.187.34 Afternoon dress, black rayon crepe, coffee-coloured machine-lace, fringed over-skirt, about 1925-28.

1967.187.35 Afternoon dress, black silk velvet devoré, apricot-coloured silk crepe insert, about 1925-28.

1967.187.36 Afternoon dress, black rayon crepe, pale grey silk crepe insert, about 1925-28.

1967.187.59 Day dress, mid-blue rayon crepe, pale grey floral machine-embroidery, about 1922-23. Cat. no. 10.

1967.187.60 Afternoon dress, chocolate-brown silk crepe, white and rust-coloured wool embroidery, labelled *44*, about 1925-28.

1967.187.61 Day dress, dark green wool gabardine, pea-green collar and cuffs, applied silver leather and gold metallic braid, labelled *44*, about 1930.

1967.187.62 Day dress, navy blue and grey silk, hand-embroidered, about 1914-16. Cat. no. 8.

1967.187.63 Day dress, blue machine-knitted rayon jersey, pale grey silk machine-embroidery, about 1914-16. Cat. no. 7.

1967.187.65 Negligée, dark blue cotton velvet, white cotton net sailor-style collar and cuffs, about 1914-20.

1967.187.69 Day dress, navy blue wool crepe, ice-blue rayon silk trimmings, about 1932-35. Cat. no. 23.

1967.187.70 Day dress, navy blue wool, blue and white spotted rayon crepe trimmings, about 1932-35.

1967.187.71 Day dress, printed cotton panne velvet, green, yellow and black speckles on a black ground. Labelled *OS, 50*, about 1930-32.

1967.187.72 Day dress, printed cotton velveteen, pale green and pink stylised flowers on a dark green ground, about 1930-32.

1967.187.72a Day dress, printed cotton velveteen, cream, red and tan-coloured stylised flowers on a blue ground, about 1930-32.

1967.187.73 Day dress, black knitted rayon jersey, white rayon satin trimmings, labelled *Melso Fabric, British Made*, about 1932-35. Cat. no. 22.

1967.187.74 Day dress, royal blue rayon crepe with grey crepe trimmings, about 1932-36.

1967.187.75 Day dress, dark blue cotton panne velvet, flesh-coloured silk crepe insert, labelled *OS, 48*, about 1930-32.

1967.187.76 Summer day dress, printed cotton and rayon crepe, floral pattern in green, white, pink, pale blue and orange on blue ground. Labelled *OS, 46*, about 1930-32. Cat. no. 19.

1967.187.77 Summer day dress, printed rayon crepe, floral pattern in orange, yellow, pale blue and cream on a mid-blue ground. Labelled *OS, 50*, about 1930-32.

1967.187.77a Summer day dress, printed rayon crepe, floral pattern in orange, yellow, pale blue and cream on a mid-blue ground. Labelled *OS, 50*, about 1930-32.

1967.187.78 Summer day dress, printed cotton and rayon crepe, stylised flower and leaf design in green, yellow, orange and white on a blue ground, labelled *Owen Owen Ltd, Liverpool, Stock No.Q25, Dept No.51, Style 4041, Size OS, Price 12/6*, and *OS, 48*, about 1930-32. Cat. no. 20.

1967.187.79 Summer day dress, printed rayon crepe, design of tulips and poppies in red, yellow, white and green on a mid-green ground, labelled *Length 48, size 48, British Make*, about 1930-32.

1967.187.80 Summer day dress, printed rayon crepe, design of daisies in red, white, pink and green on royal blue ground, labelled *Owen Owen Ltd, Liverpool, Stock No.Q22, Dept No.51, Size OS, price 20/-*, about 1930-32. Cat. no. 21.

1967.187.81 Summer day dress, printed silk crepe, floral pattern in green, pale blue, orange and white on a navy blue ground, about 1930-32. Cat. no. 18.

1967.187.82 Day dress, burgundy red cotton panne velvet, about 1930-32.

1967.187.107 Day dress, printed cotton and rayon, design of daisies in red, green, blue, white and yellow on a black ground, about 1932-35.

1967.187.109 Day dress, printed rayon crepe, chocolate brown with small white floral motif, about 1935-40.

1967.187.110 Day dress, printed rayon crepe, stylised wheatear design in white on navy blue ground, about 1935. Cat. no. 24.

1967.187.371 Tennis skirt, white cotton twill, about 1900-10.

1967.187.506 Summer day dress, pale green linen, labelled *46*, about 1925-30.

1967.187.507 Summer day dress, pale green linen, white linen collar and silk embroidery, labelled *42*, about 1925-30.

1967.187.510 Afternoon dress, black silk brocade, bodice and trained skirt, about 1890-1900. Probably belonged to Emily Tinne's mother-in-law, Deborah E. Tinne (1856-1923).

1967.187.511 Afternoon dress, dark red silk velvet devoré and silk crepe, about 1927-28. Cat. no. 16.

1967.187.512 Afternoon dress, dark red ribbed rayon, gold-coloured blonde silk lace to centre front of bodice, about 1928-30.

WAG 2001.45.3 Maternity or nursing bodice, lilac, black and white striped silk taffeta, about 1911-15. Cat. no. 1.

Other maternity clothes survive in the collection. See Cat. no. 114, and above, accession no. 1967.187.19.

WAG 2001.45.28 Tunic top, black silk and silk satin, hand-embroidered in pale blue silk and gold metallic thread. Labelled *L & M, Kom: 833, Fac: 5773, 44*. Probably made in China, for Western export, about 1923-25. Cat. no. 14.

WAG 2001.45.29 Shift dress, printed cotton polyester, psychedelic design in pink, red, green, orange, yellow and lilac, about 1967-70. Worn by Elspeth Tinne (1911-2000).

2. EVENING CLOTHES

1967.187.13 Evening dress, black silk, metallic silver braid trimming, labelled *Henry Darling & Co., Edinburgh*, about 1910. Cat. no. 25.

1967.187.16 Evening dress, black silk and silk chiffon, applied cut-steel beads, about 1914-18.

1967.187.37 Evening dress, black silk and silk crepe, trimmed with black machine-made lace, about 1925-30.

1967.187.38 Evening dress, black machine-made lace and silk satin, trimmed with black tasselled silk braid and glass bugle beads, about 1925-30.

1967.187.39 Evening dress, black cotton velvet, ruched and gathered drape of fabric at left hip, about 1925-27.

1967.187.40 Evening dress, ribbed black rayon silk, black silk fringe overskirt, about 1925-30. With matching coat, 1967.187.41. See Cat. no. 50.

1967.187.42 Evening dress, black machine-made lace, pale pink silk lining and bodice insert, about 1923-25.

1967.187.43 Evening dress, black silk machine-made lace and silk chiffon, about 1921-23. Cat. no. 26.

1967.187.44 Evening dress, black silk satin and silk crepe, centre front panel of brocaded silk and gold thread. Labelled *B, 13810, M.B. & Co, Order, Gown No., Machinist, Finisher..38 70, Size..*, about 1925-27.

1967.187.45 Evening dress, black rayon crepe, applied black glass bugle beads in floral design, about 1925-27.

1967.187.46 Evening dress, black ribbed rayon, applied black glass bugle beads, about 1925-27.

1967.187.50 Evening dress, black machine-made lace and silk crepe, circular diamanté paste brooch on left hip, about 1925-28.

1967.187.51 Evening dress, black machine-made lace, silk and silk chiffon, flower of blue, green, yellow and purple cotton velvet and wool felt applied to left hip, about 1925-28.

1967.187.52 Evening dress, black silk and silk chiffon woven with geometric rose design in silver thread, cerise pink cotton voile rosette on left hip, about 1925-27. Cat. no. 31.

1967.187.53 Evening dress, black silk and silk crepe, black glass bugle beads and plastic sequins, rosette of pink and purple silk crepe and velvet on left hip, about 1925. Cat. no. 30.

1967.187.54 Evening dress, black silk and silk crepe, black and grey glass bugle beads in large floral design. Labelled *Made in France*, about 1925. Cat. no. 28.

1967.187.55 Evening dress, black silk crepe and rayon jersey, applied black and clear glass bugle beads in a scrolling design. Labelled *Gerlaur, 33 Faubourg Poissonnière, Paris*, about 1925. Cat. no. 29.

1967.187.56 Evening dress, black silk crepe, applied silver and bronze-coloured metal beads, about 1924-25. Cat. no. 27

1967.187.57 Evening dress, black silk, black silk chiffon sleeves, applied black glass bugle beads, about 1924-25.

1967.187.58 Evening dress, black silk satin and silk crepe with chiffon sleeves, applied cut-steel beads and tiny metal rosettes in floral design, about 1925-28.

1967.187.64 Evening dress, lilac silk skirt and pale blue silk chiffon bodice over cream chiffon, draped, asymmetrical cut, about 1912.

1967.187.66 Evening dress, black silk crepe, applied silver glass bugle beads, the beaded design on centre front in the form of a bow, about 1925-28.

1967.187.83 Dinner dress and matching coatee, dark blue and black silk velvet, printed all over with tulips in cream and pale blue, about 1932-34. Cat. no. 37.

1967.187.84 Dinner dress and matching coatee, gunmetal grey silk panne velvet devoré, grey silk crepe and velvet corsage on left shoulder of coatee, about 1932-34. Cat. no. 36.

1967.187.85 Dinner dress and matching coatee, black silk crepe, raised silk velvet pile printed with flowers and fish-scale pattern in orange, yellow, blue and brown, about 1932-34. Cat. no. 35.

1967.187.86 Evening dress, black silk chiffon and velvet devoré, worked all over in a leaf pattern, about 1928-30.

1967.187.87 Evening dress, black and pale pink silk satin-backed crepe, bias cut, short train, labelled *An Olive Scott Model* and *Bon Marché, Liverpool, Ltd*, about 1935-36. Cat. no. 47.

1967.187.88 Evening dress, black silk panne velvet, figured design of palm fronds all over, large diamanté paste clasp on left hip, about 1925-28.

1967.187.89 Evening dress, black silk chiffon and velvet devoré over black silk crepe, the skirt covered with black silk fringing, about 1928-30.

1967.187.90 Evening dress, black crushed cotton velvet, circular diamanté paste brooch to bodice front, about 1932-35.

1967.187.91 Dinner dress, dusty pink silk panne velvet devoré, worked in a stylised floral pattern, about 1932-35. Cat. no. 38.

1967.187.92 Evening dress, black silk crepe, full-length and sleeveless, with black plastic sequins applied down each side, silk chiffon sleeves, about 1935-36. Cat. no. 45.

1967.187.93 Evening dress, black silk satin-backed crepe, full-length, sleeveless and bias-cut, applied clear and white glass bugle beads in circular pattern, about 1935-36. Cat. no. 46.

1967.187.94 Evening dress, black silk crepe over black silk satin, pink silk crepe yoke with panel of black plastic sequins, about 1925-28.

1967.187.95 Evening dress, black silk satin-backed crepe and silk chiffon, full-length, woven leaf motifs in silver thread to sleeves and bodice, about 1935-36. Cat. no. 44.

1967.187.96 Evening dress, black silk crepe, bias-cut skirt, draped bodice front of floral woven gold brocade, about 1932-35.

1967.187.97 Dinner dress, dark brown machine-made lace and silk crepe, lined with brown rayon satin, about 1934-36. Cat. no. 40.

1967.187.98 Dinner dress, bottle-green machine-made lace and silk crepe, about 1934-36. Cat. no. 39.

1967.187.99 Evening dress, purple rayon crepe, machine-made lace sleeves, full-length, halter neckline. Labelled *D.K. No. 3046, Style No. 954X, Size & Col. 4f, Machinist..Penny, Finisher, Presser, House ...Wain (?)*, about 1935-36. Cat. no. 43.

1967.187.101 Evening dress, black machine-made lace lined with black silk, full-length, lined with flesh-pink silk crepe and pink machine-made lace, about 1935-40.

1967.187.102 Evening dress, black rayon crepe, full-length, the bodice and sleeves of black net and crepe, about 1932-35.

1967.187.103 Evening dress and matching coatee, black machine-made lace worked in large daisy pattern, full-length, with separate black rayon taffeta under-slip. Labelled *50* and *Owen Owen Ltd, Liverpool, stock No. X18, Dept No. 11.131, Style 2432, size 50, Price 63/-.* Under-slip labelled *Machinist No.25*, about 1934-36. Cat. no. 41.

1967.197.104 Evening dress, black machine-made lace worked in large floral pattern, full-length, labelled *50*. Separate black rayon taffeta under-slip, labelled *Machinist No. 36*, about 1934-36.

1967.187.105 Evening dress and matching coatee, black machine-made lace worked in floral pattern, full-length, with puffed sleeves to coatee and separate black rayon crepe under-slip. Labelled *50* and *Owen Owen Ltd, Liverpool, Stock No.6, Dept No.131, Style 5451, Size 50, Price 63/-, 2 pce*, about 1934-36.

1967.187.106 Evening dress and matching coatee, black machine-made lace, full-length, with gilt glass buckle and separate black silk and net under-slip. Labelled *Owen Owen Ltd, Liverpool, Stock No.N15, Dept No.24, Colour No. J, Size OS, Price 94/6*, on coatee, and *Patriana* on under-slip, about 1934-36. Cat. no. 42.

1967.187.108 Evening dress, purple rayon crepe, full-length with wide, flared sleeves and diamanté paste clip to bodice front, about 1935-40.

1967.187.513 Dinner dress, dark blue silk velvet devoré, worked in floral pattern, separate under-slip of dark blue silk, about 1932-34. Cat. no. 34.

1967.187.514 Evening dress, black cotton panne velvet, full-length, wide cape-like sleeves of black silk crepe, about 1935-36.

1967.187.515 Evening dress, black silk and cotton panne velvet, figured all over with stylised poppy design, full-length, labelled *46*, about 1934-36.

1967.187.516. Evening dress, black silk georgette and machine-made lace, labelled *Owen Owen Ltd, Liverpool, Price £5.15.6, A.G., 1933, TX/Y, Tinne, Blk Geo. & Lace, A.G, 1933*

WAG 2003.11.1 Evening dress, black silk crepe over black silk, the bodice sewn with a deep V-shaped band of clear glass beads and diamanté pastes, about 1928-30.

WAG 2003.11.2 Evening dress, black silk crepe over black silk, applied iridescent glass bugle beads in a stylised floral pattern, about 1928-30. Cat. no. 33.

WAG 2003.11.3 Evening dress, black silk crepe over black silk, applied clear and black glass bugle beads and large appliquéd palm leaf motif in diamanté pastes and glass beads, about 1928-30. Cat. no. 32.

3. OUTDOOR CLOTHES AND FURS

1967.187.1 Evening cape, black silk brocade and silk velvet, applied black silk braid and ostrich feathers, about 1880-90. Probably belonged to Emily Tinne's mother-in-law, Deborah E. Tinne (1856-1923).

1967.187.2 Coat, maroon-coloured wool, collar and cuffs of brindle-coloured rabbit fur. Labelled *Cripps, Sons & Co., 12-14 & 16 Bold Street, Liverpool*, about 1925-30. Cat. no. 49.

1967.187.3 Coat, black wool, applied bands of black silk braid, collar and cuffs of beaver fur. Labelled *Cripps, Sons & Co., 12-14 & 16 Bold Street, Liverpool*, about 1925-30.

1967.187.4 Coat, black wool, collar and deep cuffs of beaver fur, about 1925-30

1967.187.5 Evening shoulder cape, black machine-made lace over finely pleated black silk. Labelled *G.H.Lee & Co. Ltd, 22 Basnett Street*, about 1900-10. Probably belonged to Emily Tinne's mother-in-law, Deborah E. Tinne (1856-1923).

1967.187.6 Coat, cream-coloured herringbone-weave wool, applied black cotton velvet and black and white silk braid, about 1912. Cat. no. 48.

1967.187.20 Duster coat, dark brown ribbed rayon, edged with rayon satin and printed silk in brown, white and orange, about 1924-25. Has matching day dress, accession number **1967.187.21**. See Cat. no. 11.

1967.187.32 Coat, royal blue ribbed silk, neckline and cuffs edged with maroon and blue printed silk. Labelled *Owen Owen Ltd, Liverpool, £12 (Price £18)*, about 1925.

1967.187.41 Evening coat, black ribbed rayon silk, the cuffs and lower half of coat decorated with white cotton machine embroidery, about 1925-30. Cat. no. 50. Has matching evening dress, 1967.187.40. See above, Evening Clothes.

1967.187.47 Evening coat, black rayon grosgrain, the lower half decorated with two deep bands of black silk fringing. Labelled *G.H.Lee & Co., Ltd, Liverpool*, about 1925-30.

1967.187.48 Evening cape, black silk crepe lined with pale green figured silk, border of black silk fringing, about 1925-30.

1967.187.49 Evening cape, black silk georgette with rows of applied, ruffled black silk satin ribbon. Labelled *Cripps, Sons & Co., 12-14 & 16 Bold Street, Liverpool*, about 1925-30. Cat. no. 63.

1967.187.67 Coat, navy blue rayon grosgrain, the collar, cuffs and front trimmed with band of navy blue rayon satin, about 1925-30.

1967.187.68 Coat, black wool crepe, partly lined with white crepe printed with black polka dots, cape-effect sleeves, about 1930-35.

1967.187.100 Shawl, deep blue silk velvet devoré on black silk crepe ground, worked in leaf design, long knotted silk fringe, about 1925-30. Cat. no. 64.

1967.187.111 Coat, black wool crepe, padded shoulders, machine-embroidered black silk leaf motifs to neckline, cuffs and front, about 1938-45. Cat. no. 71.

1967.187.112 Coat, black ribbed rayon, lined with pale grey silk, about 1925-30.

1967.187.113 Cape, blue machine-knitted rayon, worked all over in square pattern, two plaited rayon ties at neckline, about 1925-30. Cat. no. 62.

1967.187.442 Feather boa, black ostrich feathers, with black silk cord, knotted at each end, about 1920-40.

1967.187.443 Evening stole, black ostrich feathers, arranged in three parallel lengths and attached to black cotton ground, backed with black silk satin, about 1920-40.

1967.187.444 Evening stole, ivory silk, large scrolling pattern worked all over in couched gold thread, plaited silk fringe to bottom edge and sides. Probably Chinese, made for the European market, about 1920-40.

1967.187.445 Evening stole, starched cream-coloured cotton muslin, the borders and ends embroidered with Arabic letters, crescent moons and stars in gold metallic thread. Probably Egyptian, made for the European market, about 1920-40.

WAG 2001.45.1 Shoulder cape, black ribbed silk, applied black glass bugle beads and appliquéd floral motifs in lilac, green and white warp-printed silk. Labelled *G.H.Lee & Co., 22 Basnett Street, Liverpool*, about 1890-1900. Probably belonged to Emily Tinne's mother-in-law, Deborah E. Tinne (1856-1923).

WAG 2001.45.2 Shoulder cape, purple wool lined with quilted black cotton sateen, applied black silk braid, black curly fur trim to collar, about 1890-1900. Probably belonged to Emily Tinne's mother-in-law, Deborah E. Tinne (1856-1923).

WAG 2001.45.4 Coat, black sealskin, lined with black silk satin in checked pattern. Labelled *W.Creamer & Co., Ladies' Tailors, 56 Bold Street, Liverpool, Furriers by Appointment, H.M. Queen Alexandra,* and *Storage, Name…Tinne, No.83739, Date Recd. 2/7/28*, 1928. Cat. no. 54.

WAG 2001.45.5 Coat, dyed red sable, known as Kolinsky mink, worked in chevron pattern, in original box marked *Bon Marché, Liverpool (Liverpool) Ltd, Mrs Tinne (sic), Clayton Lodge, Aigburth Road, Liverpool … date 10/11/27, to be kept dry, special,* 1927. Cat. no. 52.

WAG 2001.45.6 Coat, moleskin, deep shawl collar of dyed rabbit fur. In original box marked *Owen Owen Ltd, Liverpool* and *New Mole Coat*, about 1927-30.

WAG 2001.45.7 Coat, moleskin, lined with brown rayon crepe, labelled *Scotch Mole, Satisfaction Ensured*. In original (?) box marked *Owen Owen Ltd, Liverpool*, and *Mole Coat*, about 1927-30.

WAG 2001.45.8 Coat, diamond moleskin, original silk lining now shattered and largely removed. In original box labelled *From Lewis's Ltd, Ranelagh Street, Liverpool, Mrs Tinne, Clayton Lodge, Aigburth, date 15/3/30, Dept.- Furs*, 1930. Cat. no. 58.

WAG 2001.45.9 Coat, black wool facecloth, deep collar and cuffs of beaver fur. Labelled *Cripps, Sons & Co., 12-14 & 16 Bold Street, Liverpool*, about 1926-30.

WAG 2001.45.10 Coat, black wool velour, deep collar, cuffs and trim of beaver fur. Labelled *Cripps, Sons & Co., 12-14 & 16 Bold Street, Liverpool*, about 1926-30. Cat. no. 51.

WAG 2001.45.11 Evening coat, black silk velvet, lined with white rayon silk, deep collar of white rabbit fur. Labelled *Owen Owen Ltd, Liverpool, Price 84/-*, about 1925-28.

WAG 2001.45.12 Evening mantle, black silk crepe de chine, trimmed with black marabou feathers, about 1930. Cat. no. 67.

WAG 2001.45.13 Coat, black wool facecloth, deep collar, full-length revers and cuffs all of grey chinchilla fur. Labelled *G.H.Lee & Co. Ltd, Liverpool*, about 1927-30. Cat. no. 53.

WAG 2001.45.14 Coat, black wool with woven diagonal stripe, deep collar and cuff trims of mink, about 1930. Cat. no. 56.

WAG 2001.45.15 Coat, black silk ottoman, the collar, full-length revers and cuffs all of brown moleskin. Labelled *Cripps, Sons & Co., 12-14 & 16 Bold Street, Liverpool*, about 1930. Cat. no. 55.

WAG 2001.45.16 Coat, brown nutria fur, lined with brown figured silk. Labelled *G.H.Lee & Co.Ltd, Liverpool*, about 1930. Cat. no. 59.

WAG 2001.45.17 Coat, Persian lamb, lined with black rayon silk, deep shawl collar and cuffs of beaver fur, about 1930. Cat. no. 57.

WAG 2001.45.18 Coat, antelope, lined with figured brown rayon silk, deep collar and cuffs of beaver fur. In original box labelled *Bon Marché (L.pool Ltd), The Fashion Store, Mrs Tinne, Clayton Lodge, Aigburth, Date 3/10/35*, 1935. Cat. no. 60.

WAG 2001.45.19 Coat, sealskin, lined with figured brown rayon silk, deep shawl collar and cuffs of mink, about 1930-35.

WAG 2001.45.20 Coat, Persian lamb, with deep shawl collar of mink. Labelled *Bon Marché (L.pool Ltd), The Fashion Store, Mrs Tinne, Clayton Lodge, Date 27/3/37*, 1937.

WAG 2001.45.21 Coat, sealskin, lined with figured brown rayon silk, deep shawl collar and cuffs of mink, about 1934-38. Cat. no. 61.

WAG 2001.45.22 Evening coat, black silk velvet, lined with white crepe de chine, wide pagoda sleeves, deep shawl collar of white angora rabbit fur. Labelled *G.H.Lee & Co. Ltd, Liverpool*, about 1930-36. Cat. no. 66.

WAG 2001.45.23 Duster coat, grey wool worsted, grey silk machine embroidery and glass bugle beads to shoulders and yoke. Labelled *Pure Worsted*, about 1950-58. Worn by Elspeth Tinne (1911-2000).

WAG 2001.45.24 Bridge coat, royal blue silk velvet devoré, worked in floral pattern, lined with blue silk, collar of dyed rabbit fur, about 1927-30. Cat. no. 69.

WAG 2001.45.25 Bridge coat, pink and blue silk velvet devoré worked in floral pattern, lined with pink silk, collar of dyed rabbit fur, about 1927-30. Cat. no. 68.

WAG 2001.45.26 Bridge coat, black silk panne velvet, printed with stylised palm leaf design in green and white, lined with black silk chiffon, collar of dyed rabbit fur, about 1930-34. Cat. no. 70.

WAG 2001.45.27 Evening shoulder cape, black cotton velvet, applied clear glass bugle beads. Labelled *39/6, BL, 00/-, NR*, about 1930-34. Cat. no. 65.

WAG 2001.45.30 Stole, double silver fox fur, joined together at tails, about 1930-35.

WAG 2001.45.31 Stole, double silver fox fur, joined together at single mask, backed with black silk velvet. Labelled *R/T/R, 8.8.0.(8 guineas), Silver fox*, about 1930-35. Cat. no. 81.

WAG 2001.45.32 Stole, silver fox fur, early plastic clip on under-side of mask, about 1930-35

WAG 2001.45.33 Stole, mink, sable fur tails, backed with brown rayon silk. In original (?) box marked *Owen Owen Ltd, Liverpool*, about 1930-35. Cat. no. 79.

WAG 2001.45.34 Stole, mink, sable fur tails, backed with brown rayon silk. In original (?) box marked *Owen Owen Ltd, Liverpool*, about 1930-35. Cat. no. 80.

WAG 2001.45.35 Stole, mink, backed with ruched brown silk, about 1928-32.

WAG 2001.45.36 Stole, mink, backed with brown silk crepe. In original (?) box marked *Owen Owen Ltd, Liverpool*, about 1928-32

WAG 2001.45.37 Stole, diamond moleskin, backed with figured brown rayon silk. Original receipt for £9.9.0, from Bon Marché, Church Street, Liverpool, 2 October 1926, still survives. 1926. Cat. no. 74

WAG 2001.45.38 Stole, moleskin, backed with plain brown silk. Original receipt for £8.8.0, from Bon Marché, Church Street, Liverpool, 2 October 1926, still survives, as above. 1926. Cat. no. 75

WAG 2001.45.39 Collar, moleskin, no backing, about 1925-30

WAG 2001.45.40 Cravat, ermine, backed with white silk crepe. In original box marked *From Lewis's Ltd, Ranelagh Street, Liverpool, Carriage Paid, Mrs Tinne, Clayton Lodge, Aigburth....date 5/4/33, Department – Furs*, 1933. Cat. no. 76.

WAG 2001.45.41 Stole, ermine with tails, backed with white silk crepe. In original box marked *From Lewis's Ltd, Ranelagh Street, Liverpool, Carriage Paid, Mrs Tinne, Clayton Lodge, Aigburth....date 5/4/33, Department – Furs*, 1933. Cat. no. 77.

WAG 2001.45.42 Stole, ermine, backed with white silk crepe. In original box marked *From Lewis's Ltd, Ranelagh Street, Liverpool, Carriage Paid, Mrs Tinne, Clayton Lodge, Aigburth....date 5/4/33, Department – Furs*, 1933. Cat. no. 78.

WAG 2001.45.43 Tippet, sealskin backed with black silk satin, about 1910-20.

WAG 2001.45.44 Muff, sealskin, lined with black silk satin, about 1910-15.

WAG 2001.45.46 Muff, Persian lamb, lined with black cotton sateen, about 1910-20.

WAG 2001.45.47 Stole, grey squirrel fur, dark brown sable tails at each end, backed with grey-brown silk. In original (?) box marked *Owen Owen Ltd, Liverpool*, and labelled *MR/MD 4728, 20 gns (20 guineas)*, about 1910-15. Cat. no. 72.

WAG 2001.45.48 Stole, grey squirrel fur, dark brown sable tails at each end, backed with grey and white squirrel fur. In original (?) box marked *Owen Owen Ltd, Liverpool*, and labelled *N/S/S*, about 1910-15. May be part of a pair, together with **WAG 2003.45.47**, Cat. no. 72, above.

WAG 2001.45.49 Stole, ermine with tails, backed with white silk satin. In original (?) box marked *Marten & Co., Furriers and Skin Merchants, 40 Bold Street, Liverpool, and at 235 Lord Street, Southport*, about 1910-20. Cat. no. 73.

WAG 2001.45.50 Stole, white winter fox fur, backed with white silk satin. In original box marked *Marten & Co., Furriers and Skin Merchants, 40 Bold Street, Liverpool, and at 235 Lord Street, Southport*, about 1930-35. Cat. no. 82.

WAG 2001.45.51 Stole, fox fur, backed with dark brown ruched silk satin. In original box marked *Bon Marché, Liverpool (Liverpool) Ltd, Mrs Tinne, Clayton Lodge, Aigburth, date 14/11/28. With care, to be kept dry, special*, 1928.

WAG 2001.45 52 Stole, fox fur, backed with dark brown ruched silk crepe, about 1928-32.

WAG 2001.45.53 Stole, fox fur, backed with dark brown ruched silk crepe, about 1928-32.

4. BLOUSES

1967.187.114 Blouse, white cotton muslin, with crocheted inserts and floral whitework embroidery. Labelled *AVA, 44*, about 1910-20. Cat. no. 90

1967.187.115 Blouse, white cotton muslin, with crocheted inserts, cutwork and floral whitework embroidery. Labelled *AVA, 46*, about 1910-20. Cat. no. 85

1967.187.116 Blouse, white cotton muslin, with crocheted inserts and floral whitework embroidery. Labelled *AVA, Paris Model*, about 1910-20.

1967.187.117 Blouse, ivory-coloured silk. Labelled *Size 1, The St Margaret, Regd.*, about 1910-20. Cat. no. 92.

1967.187.118 Blouse, white cotton lawn, with small warp-printed floral pattern in pale pink, pale blue and green, covered with layer of brown silk chiffon, about 1913. Cat. no. 93.

1967.187.119 Blouse, white cotton net covered with layer of navy blue silk chiffon, about 1913-15. Cat. no. 95.

1967.187.120 Blouse, white cotton net covered with layer of dark green silk chiffon, about 1913-15. Cat. no. 94.

1967.187.121 Blouse, ivory-coloured cotton muslin, cross-over front, shawl collar. Labelled *Harrod's Ltd, London, S.W., Blouse and Skirt Dept*, about 1910-20. Cat. no. 88

1967.187.122 Blouse, white cotton muslin, with floral whitework embroidery, about 1916. Cat. no. 89.

1967.187.123 Blouse, white cotton muslin, with crocheted and tape lace inserts and floral whitework embroidery. Labelled *AVA, 46*, about 1910-20. Cat. no. 84.

1967.187.124 Blouse, white cotton lawn, pin-tucks and inserted bands of needle-run net, about 1910-20.

WAG 2001.45.54 Blouse, white cotton muslin, with floral whitework embroidery. Labelled *14?* and *12/11*, about 1910-20. Cat. no. 86.

WAG 2001.45.55 Blouse, white cotton muslin, with vertical pin-tucks, drawn threadwork and floral whitework embroidery. Labelled *Paris Model* and *AVA 48*. Paper label marked *Hand-made blouses, Marque AVA, No.7287, Made in France, 2 gns*, about 1910-20. Cat. no. 91.

WAG 2001.45.56 Blouse, white cotton muslin, with machine-lace inserts and edging and floral whitework embroidery. Labelled *Louvre, Rgd. No.364484*, about 1910-20.

WAG 2001.45.57 Blouse, white cotton muslin, with drawn threadwork inserts and floral whitework embroidery. Labelled *No.1484, Size 14?, Mach'st 36, Finisher G, Order*, about 1910-20. Cat. no. 87.

WAG 2001.45.58 Blouse, white silk crepe de chine, with floral hand-embroidery in red, blue, yellow, orange, green and brown to centre front and sleeves. Labelled *Hand Embroidery, Made in Hungary*. Worn by Alexine Tinne (1923-2011), about 1933-35. Cat. no. 96.

WAG 2001.45.59 Blouse, turquoise blue cotton muslin, with cross-stitch embroidery at neckline and edges. Labelled *Made in Hungary*. Worn by Alexine Tinne (1923-2011), about 1933-35.

WAG 2001.45.60 Blouse, white cotton muslin, with cross-stitch embroidery in red silk. Worn by Alexine Tinne (1923-2011), about 1933-35.

WAG 2001.45.161 Blouse, white cotton muslin, with drawn threadwork and floral whitework embroidery, about 1910-20. Cat. no. 83.

5. UNDERWEAR AND NIGHTWEAR

1967.187.340 Camisole, white cotton, with machine-made Valenciennes lace inserts, about 1905-15. Cat. no. 102.

1967.187.341 Camisole, white cotton, with broderie anglaise trim, about 1910-20.

1967.187.342 Camisole, white cotton, with machine-made lace insertions, about 1910-20. Cat. no. 105.

1967.187.343 Camisole, white cotton, square cut with shoulder straps and whitework embroidery to centre front. Labelled *G.H.Lee & Co. Ltd, Liverpool,U.G., British & French Lingerie & Baby Linen, 4/9 and 5/6*, about 1920-30. Cat. no. 108

1967.187.344 Camisole, white cotton, square cut with pink silk ribbon shoulder straps, machine-lace trim. Labelled *G.H.Lee & Co. Ltd, Liverpool, U.G., British & French Lingerie & Baby Linen, 9/8*, about 1920-30.

1967.187.345 Camisole, white silk, machine-made lace trim, about 1910-20. Cat. no.104.

1967.187.346 Bodice, cream-coloured machine-knitted wool, short sleeves, about 1920-30.

1967.187.347 Brassière, white cotton broderie anglaise and machine-made lace. Labelled *Bien Jolie Brassière, Made in U.S.A., 15090, 40.* Made by Benjamin & Johnes, about 1920-25. Cat. no. 110.

1967.187.348 Bust bodice, white cotton, boned and laced up centre back, about 1920. Cat. no. 109.

1967.187.349 Brassière, white cotton and elasticated net, laced up centre back. Labelled *Bien Jolie Brassière, Made in U.S.A., 48/3, 36.* Made by Benjamin & Johnes, about 1920-25. Cat. no. 112.

1967.187.350 Brassière, white cotton and broderie anglaise. Labelled *Bien Jolie Brassière, Made in U.S.A., 5079, 42.* Made by Benjamin & Johnes, about 1920-25. Cat. no. 111.

1967.187.351 Drawers, closed-leg, white cotton, about 1900-20.

1967.187.352 Drawers, open-leg, white cotton, about 1900-20.

1967.187.353 Drawers, open-leg, white cotton. Labelled *E.M. Tinne* and inscribed *E.M. Tinne* in black ink, about 1910-20.

1967.187.354 Drawers, open-leg, white cotton, about 1900-20. Cat. no. 99.

1967.187.355 Drawers, closed-leg, white cotton, broderie anglaise and machine-made Valenciennes lace edging to legs, about 1900-20.

1967.187.356 Combinations, closed-leg, white cotton, buttoned flap to centre back, about 1910-20. Cat. no. 100.

1967.187.357 Combinations, open-leg, cream-coloured machine-knitted cotton. Labelled *Quality E, "Meridian", Interlock Regd., British Make.* Made by J.B. Lewis & Sons of Nottingham, about 1930-40. Cat. no. 101.

1967.187.358 Combinations, open-leg, cream-coloured machine-knitted cotton. Labelled *Quality E, "Meridian", Interlock Regd., British Make.* Made by J.B. Lewis & Sons of Nottingham, about 1930-40.

1967.187.359 Combinations, open-leg, cream-coloured machine-knitted cotton. Labelled *Quality E, "Meridian", Interlock Regd., British Make.* Made by J.B. Lewis & Sons of Nottingham, about 1930-40.

1967.187.360 Combinations, open-leg, cream-coloured machine-knitted cotton. Labelled *Quality E, "Meridian", Interlock Regd., British Make.* Made by J.B. Lewis & Sons of Nottingham, about 1930-40.

1967.187.361 Combinations, open-leg, cream-coloured machine-knitted cotton. Labelled *Quality E, "Meridian", Interlock Regd., British Make.* Made by J.B. Lewis & Sons of Nottingham, about 1930-40.

1967.187.362 Petticoat, full-length, white cotton, with broderie anglaise edgings and flounce to skirt, about 1910-20. Cat. no. 97.

1967.187.363 Petticoat, full-length, white cotton, with broderie anglaise inserts and edgings, about 1900-20.

1967.187.364 Waist petticoat, cream-coloured wool flannel, deep waistband of white cotton. Labelled *D.T.*, about 1900. Probably belonged to Emily Tinne's mother-in-law, Deborah E.Tinne (1856-1923).

1967.187.365 Waist petticoat, white cotton, deep flounce of broderie anglaise at hemline. Labelled *E.M. Tinne*, about 1910-20.

1967.187.366 Petticoat, black self-striped knitted rayon, tubular shape, elasticated bodice top. Labelled *Recenia, Ideal Artificial Silk garments, Guaranteed Ladderproof and Washable*, and *Recenia, Ideal Underwear, Regd. No. 448035, Ladderproof*, about 1920-30.

1967.187.367 Waist petticoat, black cotton sateen, deep band of accordion pleats and ruching detail to hemline, about 1910-20.

1967.187.368 Waist petticoat, black silk moiré, elasticated waistline, border of box pleats at hemline, about 1900-20.

1967.187.369 Waist petticoat, checked silk moiré, in blue, green, black and white, band of accordion pleats at hemline, about 1910-20.

1967.187.370 Waist petticoat, petrol blue silk taffeta, four rows of ruffled pleats to hemline, about 1910-20.

1967.187.372 Corselette, white cotton canvas, seven long and short straps to centre front, the silver metal buttons stamped *Our Own Make*, about 1920-30.

1967.187.373 Nightdress, full-length, cream-coloured wool flannel. Labelled *E.M.Tinne*, about 1910-20.

1967.187.374 Nightdress, full-length, white cotton, machine-made lace insertions. Labelled *E.M. Tinne*, about 1910-20.

1967.187.375 Nightdress, full-length, white cotton, broderie anglaise ruffles to collar and cuffs. Labelled *E.McC*, about 1900-10. Belonged to Emily Tinne before her marriage, when she was still Emily McCulloch.

1967.187.376 Nightdress, full-length, white cotton, broderie anglaise ruffles to collar and cuffs, about 1900-10. Cat. no. 115.

1967.187.377 & 377a Nightdress, full-length, cream-coloured wool flannel, both sleeves detached but present, about 1910-20.

1967.187.378 Bed jacket, white cotton, wrap-over style, broderie anglaise and machine-made lace trim. Labelled *E.M. Tinne*, about 1910-20. Cat. no. 118.

1967.187.379 Bed jacket, white cotton lawn, small gores beneath arms, broderie anglaise and lace trim. Labelled *M. Tinne*, about 1910-20. Cat. no. 117.

1967.187.380 Bed jacket, white cotton lawn, small gores beneath arms, machine-made Valenciennes lace trim. Labelled *M. Tinne*, about 1910-20.

1967.187.381 Dressing gown, full-length, white figured cotton, woven all over with spot motif, broderie anglaise trim, about 1910-20. Cat. no. 116.

1967.187.382 Dressing gown, full-length, pale pink wool flannel, originally machine-sewn, now in 15 separate pieces, about 1910-20.

1967.187.407 Petticoat, calf-length, white cotton, square-cut, embroidered floral cutwork to bodice and skirt front. Labelled *No. 14716, 48, Made in France*, and *G.H.Lee & Co. Ltd, Liverpool, U.G., British and French Lingerie & Baby Linen, 7/11*, about 1920-30. Cat. no. 98.

1967.187.467 Petticoat, calf-length, flesh-coloured knitted rayon. Labelled *Best Quality British Celanese Ltd, Locknit Fabric, "Macrea", Size O.S.*, about 1920-30.

1967.187.468 Chemisette, white silk satin, vevet ribbon trim, about 1920-40.

1967.187.478 Camisole, white cotton, broderie anglaise and machine-made lace inserts. Inscribed *E.M. Tinne* in black ink, about 1910-20.

1967.187.479 Camisole, white cotton, machine-made lace inserts, pin-tucks. Labelled *Sterling, £, Lock Stitch, Trademark, S & S*, and inscribed *H.M. McCulloch* in black ink. Made by Stapley and Smith of London Wall, about 1905-10.

1967.187.480 Camisole, white cotton, machine-made lace inserts and pin-tucks. Labelled *E.M. Tinne*, about 1910-20.

1967.187.481 Camisole, white cotton lawn, machine-made Valenciennes lace inserts and pin-tucks, about 1905-15.

1967.187.482 Camisole, white cotton lawn, torchon lace inserts, whitework embroidery and pin-tucks. Labelled *Owen Owen Ltd, Liverpool, 12/6D*, about 1910-20. Cat. no. 103.

1967.187.483 Camisole, white cotton, machine-made Valenciennes lace inserts, floral whitework embroidery and pin-tucks. Labelled *E.M. Tinne*, about 1910-20.

1967.187.484 Camisole, pale blue cotton, machine-made Valenciennes lace inserts. Labelled *Owen Owen Ltd, Liverpool, 6/11*, about 1910-20.

1967.187.485 Camisole, pale pink cotton, machine-made Valenciennes lace inserts. Labelled *Owen Owen Ltd, Liverpool, 6/11*, about 1910-20. Cat. no.106.

1967.187.486 Camisole, white cotton, floral whitework embroidery and pin-tucks. Labelled *50* and stamped *411, 50*, about 1910-20.

1967.187.487 Brassière, white cotton lace, V-shaped neckline with pale pink silk satin rosette at top. Stamped *Bien Jolie Brassière, Made in U.S.A., 1500, 40*. Made by Benjamin and Johnes, about 1920-25.

1967.187.488 Drawers, open-leg, white cotton. Labelled *D.E. Tinne*, about 1900. Belonged to Emily Tinne's mother-in-law, Deborah E. Tinne (1856-1923).

1967.187.489 Drawers, open-leg, white cotton, back-fastening with two linen-covered buttons, about 1900-20.

1967.187.490 Drawers, open-leg, white cotton. Embroidered *T*, about 1900-20.

1967.187.491 Drawers, closed-leg, white cotton. Embroidered *Tinne*, about 1900.

1967.187.492 Drawers, open-leg, white cotton. Labelled *D.E. Tinne*, about 1900. Belonged to Emily Tinne's mother-in-law, Deborah E. Tinne (1856-1923).

1967.187.493 Drawers, open-leg, white cotton. Labelled *D.E. Tinne*, about 1900. Belonged to Emily Tinne's mother-in-law, Deborah E. Tinne (1856-1923).

1967.187.494 Waist petticoat, white sprigged cotton muslin, deep flounce from below knee. Labelled *E.M. Tinne*, about 1910-20.

WAG 2001.45.61 Petticoat, full-length, white cotton, dropped waistline, floral whitework embroidery to bodice front, about 1925-30.

WAG 2001.45.62 Bed jacket, cream wool cashmere, trimmed with machine-made Valenciennes lace, about 1910-20.

WAG 2001.45.63 Bed jacket, cream wool cashmere, trimmed with machine-made Valenciennes lace, about 1910-20.

WAG 2001.45.64 Camisole, white cotton. Labelled *E.M. Tinne* in red, and inscribed *E.M. Tinne* in black ink, about 1920. Cat. no. 107.

WAG 2001.45.65 Camisole, ivory silk, straps of machine-made lace threaded with pale pink silk ribbon. Labelled *4/11*, about 1910-20.

WAG 2001.45.66 Corset, probably made for playing sport, white cotton net, lacing up centre back, two elasticated suspenders to centre front. Inscribed *1414 3* in pencil, about 1900-05. Cat. no. 113.

WAG 2001.45.67 Corset, flesh-coloured nylon, elasticated inserts, top section of bra-cups of machine-embroidered net, imitating lace. Labelled *Welfia*, about 1950-60 Belonged to Elspeth Tinne (1911-2000).

WAG 2003.11.4 Maternity corset, white cotton twill, elasticated panels, lacing up centre back and both sides. Stamped *La Mère*, and *British Make*, about 1920. Cat. no. 114.

Other maternity clothes survive in the collection. See Cat. no.1, and above, Day Clothes, accession no. 1967.187.19

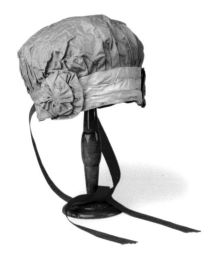

6. SWIMWEAR

1967.187.383 Woman's bathing costume, navy blue machine-knitted cotton jersey, short overskirt, about 1915-20. Cat. no. 122.

1967.187.384 Woman's bathing costume, navy blue machine-knitted cotton jersey. Labelled *L8-8422* and *Made in England, St Margaret Regd.*, about 1920.

1967.187.385 Woman's bathing costume, navy blue machine-knitted cotton jersey, about 1920-25. Cat. no. 123.

1967.187.386 Woman's bathing costume, navy blue and red machine-knitted cotton jersey with overskirt. Labelled *L8-8422* and *St Margaret, Encora, Made in England*, about 1915-20.

1967.187.387 Woman's bathing costume, black machine-knitted cotton jersey, the left-hand side worked in blue and yellow horizontal stripes. Labelled *Meridian Regd., Interlock, The Perfect Fabric for Sensitive Skins, British Make. After bathing rinse well in clear fresh water. Restore to normal shape before drying. Sensola*. Made by J.B. Lewis & Sons of Nottingham, about 1925-30. Cat. no. 124.

1967.187.388a & b Woman's two-piece bathing costume, red-orange wool serge tunic and bathing knickers, the tunic with white wool serge sailor collar. Labelled *L.Y. & J. Nathan, 4 Hardman Street, Liverpool*. Worn by Emily Tinne during her honeymoon in Ireland, 1910. Cat. no. 119.

1967.187.471 Woman's bathing costume, navy blue machine-made cotton jersey, large sailor collar, about 1920-25.

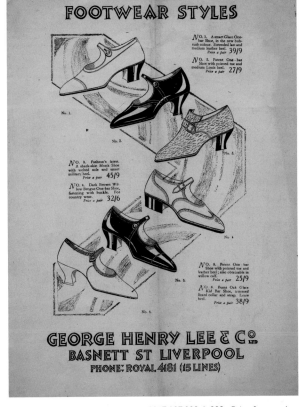

7. SHOES

1967.187.216 Pair of women's boots, black leather, ankle-length, lace-ups, about 1910-20. Cat. no. 131.

1967.187.217 Pair of women's shoes, black glacé kid leather. Stamped *Norvic* inside, and *Norvic, Shoes for Ladies, Cash Price 32/6* on the leather soles, about 1920. Cat. no. 132.

1967.187.218 Pair of women's shoes, black patent leather, the vamps edged with pinky-brown punched leather. Stamped *Helen Shoe* on the leather soles and labelled *9.34, 8/11*, about 1934. Cat. no. 136.

1967.187.219 Pair of women's shoes, grey leather, applied strips of pale pink leather, about 1927-30. Cat. no. 137.

1967.187.220 Pair of women's shoes, tan-coloured leather. Stamped *J.Collinson & Co, Bold Street, Liverpool, Chester, Wrexham*, about 1923-26. Cat. no. 134.

1967.187.221 Pair of women's shoes, black leather, elasticated side-vents, small cut-steel buckles, about 1915-20. Cat. no. 129.

1967.187.222 Pair of women's shoes, black leather, elasticated side-vents, small cut-steel buckles, about 1915-20.

1967.187.223 & 223a Pair of women's shoes, black glacé kid leather, pierced metal buckles set with cut-steel beads. Stamped *Lotus Midform, British Made*. In original shoebox, labelled *Lotus, British Made, Glacé Black Kid, 6?, Midform*, and *Delta Shoes, Lotus Shoes*, about 1920. Cat. no. 133.

1967.187.224 Pair of women's shoes, black suede, elasticated side-vents, small cut-steel rosettes. Labelled *Norvic, The Shoe De Luxe*, and stamped *Norvic, Shoes for Ladies* on the leather soles, about 1915-20. Cat. no. 130.

1967.187.225 Pair of women's shoes, dark brown glacé kid leather, cut-steel and bronze beads to vamp and strap. Stamped *The Imperial, Regd. No.48340*, about 1910-15. Cat. no. 127.

1967.187.226 Pair of women's shoes, black glacé kid leather, cut-away vamps with black glass beads, about 1910-15. Cat. no. 126.

1967.187.227 Pair of women's shoes, black glacé kid leather, applied black glass beads, about 1910-15.

1967.187.228 Pair of women's court shoes, black glacé kid leather, black petersham ribbon bows on vamps. Stamped *J.Collinson & Co., 34 & 36 Bold Street, Liverpool*, about 1910-15. Cat. no. 128.

1967.187.229 Pair of women's shoes, black glacé kid leather. Stamped *Brit-Ban* and *The Brit-Ban, Regd*, about 1925-28.

1967.187.230 Pair of women's evening shoes, black cotton sateen, strap and button across instep, the button set with diamanté pastes. Labelled *Thièrry, est.1839, Military Bootmaker, Bold St, Liverpool,* and stamped *G.Thièrry, 5 Bold St, Liverpool,* about 1923-26. Cat. no. 135.

1967.187.231 Pair of women's shoes, white kid leather, about 1925-30.

1967.187.232 Pair of women's court shoes, black wool gabardine, pewter buckle set with diamanté pastes on the vamp, about 1930-32. Cat. no. 138.

1967.187.233 Pair of women's shoes, black glacé kid leather, oval-shaped gilt metal buckles set with diamanté pastes. Stamped *Made in Paris for W.H. Watts & Co. Ltd, Boot and Shoe Importers, Liverpool,* about 1910-15. Cat. no. 125.

1967.187.234a Pair of women's court shoes, royal blue cotton sateen, squared toes, ruffled sateen bows on vamps, about 1850-60.

1967.187.388d Pair of women's espadrilles, white linen uppers, soles of coiled jute, embroidered with anchors in red wool. Worn by Emily Tinne during her honeymoon in Ireland, 1910. Cat. no. 121.

1967.187.502 Pair of men's ankle-length boots, black leather, buttoning up sides. Stamped *T.K. Fleming & Son Ltd, North John Street, Liverpool,* about 1880-1900. With pair of adjustable wooden shoe trees, stamped *Sorosis. Sorosis* was a tradename used by the Saxone Shoe Co. Ltd. In brown leather case, stamped *H.W.T.* Belonged to Philip Tinne's uncle, Herman William Tinne (1853-1937).

1967.187.504 Seven shoe bags, natural-coloured linen, drawstring tops, for the protection and storage of shoes. Labelled *L.B. Tinne* and *T,* embroidered *Tinne* and inscribed *H.W. Tinne.* Belonged to Philip Tinne's uncle, Herman William Tinne (1853-1937) and his wife, Lucy Byng Tinne, née Livingstone.

WAG 2003.11.8 Pair of women's shoes, brown leather lace-ups, small stamped leather inserts to the facings. Stamped *Begonia Shoe* on the leather soles, about 1935-40. Cat. no. 140.

WAG 2003.11.9 Pair of women's court shoes, black glacé kid leather, high heels, lizard-skin strap and buckle to front of vamps. Stamped *Lewis's, Liverpool, Manchester, Leeds, Birmingham, Glasgow,* about 1932-36.

WAG 2003.11.10 Pair of women's court shoes, brown glacé kid leather, high heels, lizard-skin strap and buckle to front of vamps. Stamped *Lewis's, Liverpool, Manchester, Leeds, Birmingham, Glasgow* and *Non-slip heels,* about 1932-36. Cat. no. 139.

WAG 2003.11.11 Pair of women's court shoes, grey glacé kid leather, high heels, lizard-skin strap and buckle to front of vamps. Stamped *Lewis's, Liverpool, Manchester, Leeds, Birmingham, Glasgow* and *Non-slip heels,* about 1932-36.

8. HATS

1967.187.204 Woman's sun bonnet, pale blue cotton, the crown and brim both shaped by cording, gathered cotton neckshield at centre back, about 1900-15. Cat. no. 141.

1967.187.205 Young girl's sun bonnet, pale blue cotton, lined with cotton tarlatan for support, corded brim, narrow, gathered neck-shield, about 1900-15.

1967.187.250 Woman's hat, black silk velour, trimmed with curled egret feathers. Labelled *Millinery Bon Marché, (Liverpool) Ltd,* about 1918-22. Cat. no. 145.

1967.187.251 Woman's hat, brown horsehair, known as crin, decorated with garland of cotton velvet and mother-of-pearl flowers, about 1918-22. Cat. no. 159.

1967.187.252 Woman's hat, black horsehair, known as crin, covered with black silk net and machine-made lace, garland of pink and lilac silk roses, about 1918-22. Cat. no. 160.

1967.187.253 Woman's hat, black silk covered with black silk net and machine-made lace, about 1920.

1967.187.254 Woman's hat, dark navy blue straw, decorated with garland of blue cotton velvet flowers, about 1920-24. Cat. no. 157.

1967.187.255 Woman's hat, black silk velour, trimmed with curled bird of paradise feathers. Labelled *Millinery Bon Marché (Liverpool) Ltd,* about 1923-25.

1967.187.256 Woman's hat, black horsehair, known as crin, covered with black silk net, trimmed with black bird of paradise feathers. Labelled *George Henry Lee & Co.Ltd, Basnett Street, Liverpool,* about 1912-18.

1967.187.257 Woman's hat, black silk velour, trimmed with black ostrich feather. Labelled *Madame Val Smith Ltd, Liverpool,* about 1918-22. Cat. no. 143.

1967.187.258 Woman's hat, black horsehair, known as crin, trimmed with egret feathers. Labelled *George Henry Lee & Co. Ltd, Basnett Street, Liverpool,* about 1924-26. Cat. no. 147.

1967.187.259 Woman's hat, black silk velour, decorated with wing of dyed black cock's feathers, edged with silver paint. Labelled *Millinery Bon Marché (Liverpool) Ltd,* about 1918-20.

1967.187.260 Woman's hat, decorated with dark blue silk cockade, about 1924-28.

1967.187.261 Woman's hat, black silk net, decorated with large ruffled silk net rosette, about 1918-22. Cat. no. 144.

1967.187.262 Woman's hat, natural woven straw, decorated with large embroidered raffia flowers and leaves in purple, green and yellow, about 1920-24.

1967.187.263 Woman's hat, natural woven straw, decorated with large embroidered raffia flowers and butterfly in green, orange, purple and cream, about 1920-24. Cat. no. 156.

1967.187.264 Woman's hat, black corded silk, crown swathed with silk satin and trimmed with woven horsehair braid, known as crin, and with black celluloid brooch set with diamanté pastes, about 1925.

1967.187.265 Woman's hat, black horsehair, known as crin, decorated on one side with large applied rosette of twisted black silk satin ribbon, about 1925-27. Cat. no. 150.

1967.187.266 Woman's hat, black straw, decorated with applied pink feather 'flowers'. Labelled *Millinery Bon Marché (Liverpool) Ltd,* about 1925-27.

1967.187.267 Woman's hat, black wool felt, pinched and moulded crown with feather-shaped marcasite brooch at centre front. Stamped *Henry Heath Ltd, By Special Appointment to His Majesty the King, Established in the reign of King George IV, 1822,* and labelled *7 1/4* and *27,* about 1925-27.

1967.187.268 Woman's hat, dark blue silk satin and corded silk, about 1925-27.

1967.187.269 Woman's cloche hat, dark brown wool felt, brim of fine, woven brown straw, folded back over crown. Labelled *Cripps, Sons & Co., 12, 14 & 16 Bold Street, Liverpool,* about 1929-31. Cat. no. 171.

1967.187.270 Woman's cloche hat, fine, pale green straw, brim folded back at centre front. Stamped *A Craven Hat* and labelled *Cripps, Sons & Co., 12, 14 & 16 Bold Street, Liverpool,* about 1928-31. Cat. no. 169.

1967.187.271 Woman's cloche hat, shiny black straw, decorated with applied silver sequins and silver thread, about 1928-30. Cat. no. 167.

1967.187.272 Woman's hat, black straw, decorated with black silk satin ribbon and bow. Labelled *7 1/2,* about 1933-35.

1967.187.273 Woman's hat, black horsehair, known as crin, cap shape, no brim, applied leaves of black and cream cotton velvet, about 1932-35.

1967.187.274 Woman's hat, black straw, decorated with pleated black silk petersham ribbon, black and white cotton organza flower heads and black silk net, about 1932-35.

1967.187.275 Woman's cocktail hat, black horsehair, known as crin, three orange-red plastic ball-beads applied to crown, about 1932-35. Cat. no. 183.

1967.187.276 Woman's hat, shiny black straw, garland of cotton velvet flowers in pink, blue and white, about 1932-35. Cat. no. 179.

1967.187.277 Woman's hat, fine brown straw, two applied, overlapping leaf shapes of brown cotton velvet to centre front. Stamped *A Mortimer Hat* and labelled *Cripps, Sons & Co., 12, 14 & 16 Bold Street, Liverpool*, about 1926-28. Cat. no. 165.

1967.187.278 Woman's cloche hat, shiny green straw, crown with deep, swathed band of gold silk satin. Stamped *A Payzway Hat* and labelled *Cripps, Sons & Co., 12, 14 & 16 Bold Street, Liverpool*, about 1925-28. Cat. no. 164.

1967.187.279 Woman's hat, pale grey horsehair, known as crin, applied bunch of small pink, lilac and blue velvet flowers beneath left side of brim. Stamped *Forest Hat, Made in England*, about 1932-35.

1967.187.280 Woman's hat, black silk velour, applied band of black egret feathers. Labelled *Millinery, Bon Marché (Liverpool) Ltd*, about 1925-27.

1967.187.280a Woman's cloche hat, blue, green, brown and purple straw. Labelled *Bon Marché (Liverpool) Ltd, Sale, 8/-*, about 1923-26.

1967.187.281 Woman's hat, plain black silk, applied band of black egret feathers. Labelled *Connor Hat, Made in England, Registered*, about 1925-27.

1967.187.281a Woman's hat, mauve, green and yellow woven straw, crown swathed with green paisley-printed cotton. Stamped *A Stuarson Hat* and labelled *Stuarson Hats, 378-33, AO, 121* and *No.dfl*, about 1922-24. Cat. no. 163.

1967.187.282 Woman's hat, black straw, applied band of black machine lace and woven straw braid. Stamped *A Raymonde Hat, Made in England*, about 1925.

1967.187.283 Woman's hat, black silk velour and corded silk, high, swathed crown. Labelled *Owen Owen Ltd, Liverpool*, about 1925-27.

1967.187.284 Woman's hat, black silk velvet, decorated at centre front with long pewter arrow-shaped brooch, set with diamanté pastes, about 1925.

1967.187.285 Woman's hat, black straw, decorated with folded black silk satin, corded silk triangles edged with black horsehair, known as crin, and triangular-shaped white metal brooch, about 1924-26. Cat. no. 148.

1967.187.286 Woman's hat, black silk velour, band of black silk velvet and large circular ribbon rosette, the centre set with tiny silver metal studs, about 1924-26. Cat. no. 149.

1967.187.287 Woman's hat, black straw, two large applied flowers in beige cotton velvet. Labelled *Millinery Bon Marché (Liverpool) Ltd*, about 1925-27. Cat. no. 151.

1967.187.288 Woman's hat, fine pinky-brown straw, applied ostrich feathers, dyed pinky-brown. Labelled *George Henry Lee & Co. Ltd, Liverpool*, about 1926-28.

1967.187.289 Woman's hat, navy blue straw, crown covered with navy blue silk satin, decorated with three applied satin flower heads, about 1922-25.

1967.187.290 Woman's hat, navy blue horsehair, known as crin, decorated across centre front with pleated and swathed navy blue silk moiré ribbon, about 1925-27.

1967.187.291 Woman's hat, brown straw, decorated with deep, ruffled flounce of brown machine-made lace and brown celluloid brooch, set with diamanté pastes, about 1925-27. Cat. no. 161.

1967.187.292 Woman's hat, brown horsehair, known as crin, brim of shiny brown straw, applied 'leaves' of brown cotton velvet. Stamped *The Orb Make, Highest Grade*, about 1930-32. Cat. no. 177.

1967.187.293 Woman's hat, fine navy blue straw, decorated with navy blue silk velvet ribbon and large bow on left side. Stamped *De Moysey, 17 rue de L'Echiquier, Paris* and *Ranelagh Street, Liverpool*, about 1928-30. Cat. no. 173.

1967.187.294 Woman's hat, fine pale grey straw, decorated with grey silk petersham ribbon, bow and silvered metal ring at centre back, about 1930-32. Cat. no. 176.

1967.187.295 Woman's cloche hat, dark brown wool felt, the rounded crown set with two inverted V-shapes in silk plush. Labelled *Cripps, Sons & Co., 12, 14 & 16 Bold Street, Liverpool*, about 1929-30.

1967.187.296 Woman's hat, mid-green wool felt, band of green silk petersham ribbon set with a green and cream wooden ring at centre front, about 1932-35.

1967.187.297 Young girl's hat, dark brown wool felt, crown with integrated band of woven straw, striped pale green, yellow and brown, about 1930-32. Worn by one of the Tinne girls as a teenager. Cat. no. 174.

1967.187.298 Woman's hat, purple straw, with applied purple silk satin ribbon and bunches of violets in pink and purple cotton velvet, above and beneath brim. Stamped *De Moysey, 17 rue de L'Echiquier, Paris* and *Ranelagh Street, Liverpool*, about 1932-35.

1967.187.299 Woman's hat, black wool felt, folded and pinched brim of black woven straw, decorated with small flower heads in black and white cotton velvet. Stamped *De Moysey, 17 rue de L'Echiquier, Paris* and *Ranelagh Street, Liverpool*, about 1932-35.

1967.187.300 Woman's cloche hat, chocolate brown wool felt, decorated with two large applied feathers, dyed cream and brown, on a cotton ground. Labelled *Cripps, Sons & Co., 12, 14 & 16 Bold Street, Liverpool*, about 1928-30. Cat. no. 172.

1967.187.301 Woman's hat, fine blue straw, crown wrapped with printed cotton scarf in blue, black, orange and cream. Stamped *The Daelyne, Regd., British Make*, about 1924-26. Cat. no. 162.

1967.187.302 Young girl's hat, yellow straw and wool, band of yellow silk petersham ribbon. Stamped *Reslaw Hat*, about 1930-32. Worn by one of the Tinne girls as a teenager. Cat. no. 175.

1967.187.303 Woman's hat, natural straw, decorated with garland of dried grasses and artificial flowers in red, yellow and green, about 1918-20. Cat. no. 155.

1967.187.304 Woman's hat, beige-coloured raffia, garland of artificial wild flowers in pink, yellow and green silk, about 1932-35. Cat. no. 181.

1967.187.305 Young girl's hat, black wool felt, crown with integrated band of woven straw, striped cream, red and black, about 1930-32. Worn by one of the Tinne girls as a teenager.

1967.187.306 Woman's hat, dark brown wool velour, decorated with dark brown moiré silk ribbon and small dyed pink feathers. Labelled *George Henry Lee & Co. Ltd, Basnett Street, Liverpool*, about 1932-35.

1967.187.307 Woman's hat, navy blue wool velour, sloping, angled brim, rounded crown decorated with applied feathers, alternating blue and white. Stamped *Peacock Hat, Regd., British Manufacture*, about 1932-35.

1967.187.308 Woman's hat, dark brown wool velour, two ruched and applied bands of red and brown silk velvet, twisted together. Embroidered *Reslaw Hat*, about 1932-35. Cat. no. 178.

1967.187.309 Woman's hat, pale grey wool velour, applied cock's feathers dyed pale pink and purple. Labelled *Jonedom Millinery, Rgd.*, about 1935-37.

1967.187.310 Woman's hat, coffee-coloured woven fibre (?), large cotton velvet flowers in pale grey, blue, lilac, brown and gold, about 1925-27. Cat. no. 152.

1967.187.311 Woman's hat, dark brown straw, deep, pleated band of dark brown rayon satin and applied silk braid triangles, about 1927-28. Cat. no. 166.

1967.187.312 Woman's hat, black horsehair, known as crin, crown swathed with black silk crepe, the crown and brim both embroidered with stylised leaves in pale pink and brown silk. Labelled *13/11* (price), about 1926-27. Cat. no. 153.

1967.187.313 Woman's hat, brown wool felt, band of brown felt and triangular-shaped plastic clip at centre front. Stamped *The "Cross Keys" Hat*, about 1928-30.

1967.187.314 Woman's cloche hat, mid-blue wool felt, both crown and brim decorated all over with parallel lines of machine-stitching in pale blue, about 1928-30.

1967.187.315 Woman's hat, navy blue wool felt, decorated with two bands of navy blue cotton velvet and dyed navy blue feathers. Labelled *Millinery, G.H. Lee and Co. Ltd, Liverpool*, about 1932-35.

1967.187.316 Woman's hat, chocolate brown cotton velvet, turned back brim sewn with parallel lines of stitching, soft, rounded crown with deep band of brown silk ribbon, about 1922-24.

1967.187.317 Woman's hat, navy blue wool felt, navy blue silk petersham band and small, dyed navy blue ostrich feathers, about 1935-40.

1967.187.318 Woman's hat, navy blue straw, decorated with navy blue silk petersham ribbon, about 1935-40.

1967.187.319 Woman's boater-style hat, fine navy blue straw, wide shallow crown decorated with pleated band of white silk petersham ribbon. Labelled *Modèles Luzy, Paris*, about 1935-39. Cat. no. 185.

1967.187.320 Woman's hat, shiny brown straw, rolled band of cream silk ribbon and brown straw, both crown and brim sewn with parallel lines in triangles. Stamped *Paulette*, about 1932-35. Cat. no. 182.

1967.187.321 Woman's hat, shiny brown straw, crown decorated with large cream rayon silk flower head. Stamped *"Yeltrow" Comfort Fitting Hat, Regd.*, about 1932-35. Cat. no. 180.

1967.187.322 Woman's hat, natural straw, decorated with navy blue silk satin and applied purple cotton velvet pansies. Labelled *K. & A.Lennon,Milliners and Costumiers, 349 Aigburth Road, Liverpool & 170 Poulton Road, Seacombe*, about 1910-20. Cat. no. 154.

1967.187.323 Woman's hat, natural straw, covered with layers of black and white silk chiffon, wide brim, black above, white below, garland of white cotton roses and leaves, about 1907-12.

1967.187.324 Woman's beret, black wool felt bound with black silk ribbon and felt decoration, about 1945-50.

1967.197.324a Woman's hat, black straw, black net veil, garland of dried grasses and artificial wild flowers in pink cotton velvet. Stamped *The "Fountain" Hat*, about 1932-35.

1967.187.325 Woman's hat, navy blue shiny straw, finely pleated and applied navy blue and white silk petersham ribbon. Labelled *Owen Owen Ltd, Liverpool, 12/9* (crossed out), *6/3* (reduced price), about 1935-36. Cat. no. 184.

1967.187.326 Woman's hat, black straw, black silk petersham ribbon and fanned cockade of ribbed silk, circular diamanté paste ring, about 1935-40.

1967.187.327 Woman's hat, black silk velvet, the soft shallow crown and brim both sewn all over with decorative stitching in geometric design, about 1935-40.

1967.187.328 Woman's hat, black silk velvet, applied black silk petersham ribbon, about 1910-20.

1967.187.329 Woman's hat, black straw, decorated with black cotton velvet knotted and pleated on right-hand side, about 1926-27.

1967.187.330 Woman's hat, shiny black straw, rolled bands of purple and lilac ribbed silk and posy of artificial flowers in pink, blue and green cotton velvet, about 1932-35.

1967.187.331 Woman's hat, shiny navy blue straw, large bow of navy blue silk petersham ribbon, held at centre back with yellow plastic clip. Stamped *Reslaw Hat* and labelled *Owen Owen Ltd, Liverpool, 12/9* (crossed out), *5/-* (reduced price), about 1932-36.

1967.187.332 Woman's hat, black horsehair, known as crin, decorated with black silk petersham ribbon and bow of black and cream silk petersham. Stamped *Lystalite, Cannon Make, Regd.*, about 1932-35.

1967.187.333 Woman's hat, black straw, black silk net veil, with two ruched and applied black silk crepe motifs at centre front, about 1925.

1967.187.334 Woman's hat, coffee-coloured wool crepe, elliptical-shaped brim, turned up at left-hand side and decorated with applied coffee-coloured silk ribbon arranged in concentric circles, about 1922-24. Cat. no. 146.

1967.187.335 Woman's hat, black silk plush, deep band and bow of black silk plush. Stamped *A Gresham Hat, Regd., Best British Make*, about 1935-40.

1967.187.335a Woman's cloche hat, emerald green wool felt, turned-back brim, moulded circular crown with applied felt bow, about 1929-31.

1967.187.335b Woman's hat, sage green woven straw, applied ribbed silk ribbon. Stamped *The Morsward Hat*, about 1922-24.

1967.187.335c Woman's hat, woven raspberry pink fibre, wide ribbon and large floppy bow of raspberry pink silk velvet, about 1922-24.

1967.187.388c Woman's bathing cap, orange rubberised cotton sateen, shallow crown gathered on to band around forehead, cotton sateen rosette over each ear, woven red wool tape ties. Worn by Emily Tinne during her honeymoon in Ireland, 1910. Cat. no. 120.

1967.187.472 Woman's cloche hat, brown wool felt, middle section of crown of woven brown straw. Stamped *A Craven Hat, Regd.* and labelled *Cripps, Sons & Co, 12, 14 & 16 Bold Street, Liverpool*, about 1928-31. Cat. no. 170.

1967.187.473 Woman's cloche hat, pale green straw, crown with green wool felt insert and felt ribbon with gilt metal buckle to right-hand side. Labelled *Cripps, Sons & Co, 12 14 & 16 Bold Street, Liverpool*, about 1928-31. Cat. no. 168.

1967.187.500 Man's rectangular top hat case, brown leather, lined with red cotton and padded with red cotton sateen, with brass lock to lid and thick leather handle. Labelled *Army & Navy Co-Operative Society Ltd, A & NCSL, 105 Victoria St, Westminster, S.W., Made at the Society's Works* and stamped *H.W.T.* on the lid, about 1880-1900. Belonged to Philip Tinne's uncle, Herman William Tinne (1853-1937).

1967.187.501a Man's top hat, black silk, with black wool felt hatband, the brim bound with black silk petersham ribbon. Stamped *Extra Quality* and *Walter Barnard & Son, 97 Jermyn St, St James's, London*, about 1880-1900. Belonged to Philip Tinne's uncle, Herman William Tinne (1853-1937).

1967.187.501b Man's top hat band, used for mourning, a long length of black cotton sateen, gathered into flat knot at each end, to be wrapped around top hat, about 1880-1900. Belonged to Philip Tinne's uncle, Herman William Tinne (1853-1937).

WAG 2001.45.45 Woman's motoring bonnet, sealskin lined with dark brown silk satin, large rosette of printed cotton, covered with black silk chiffon, over each ear, long veil of dark brown silk chiffon, ribbons of dark brown silk faille, about 1910-15. Cat. no.142.

WAG 2001.45.146 Woman's cloche hat, claret red wool velour, the folded-back brim lined with a lighter shade of red velour. Stamped *A Payzway Hat* and labelled *Cripps, Sons & Co, 12, 14 & 16 Bold Street, Liverpool*, about 1928-1931.

WAG 2001.45.147 Woman's hat, brown wool felt, soft, asymmetric brim, rounded crown with band and bow of brown silk velvet, about 1932-35.

WAG 2001.45.148 Woman's hat, mid-brown wool felt, large quatrefoil shape in concentric circles of white cotton stitching. Labelled *Trikki, by Edna Wallace, Paris*, about 1960-65.

WAG 2001.45.149 Woman's hat, natural woven straw, deep band of dark brown cotton velvet and large bow at centre back, about 1920-24. Cat. no. 158.

WAG 2001.45.150 Woman's hat, dark brown woven fibre (?) tape lace, deep floppy brim, rounded crown, no lining, about 1930-35.

WAG 2001.45.151 Woman's hat, mid-brown woven fibre (?) tape lace, deep floppy brim, rounded crown, no lining, about 1930-35.

WAG 2001.45.152 Woman's hat, grass green straw, tri-lobed shape, moulded to head, the crown decorated with applied bunches of artificial flowers, about 1953-55.

WAG 2001.45.153 Young woman's hat, pale green and yellow woven straw tape, wide turned-up brim, rounded crown with olive green silk petersham band. Labelled *Otto Lucas, Junior*, about 1958-63.

WAG 2001.45.154 Woman's 'baker boy' style hat, dark brown nylon velour, sewn all over in diaper pattern, soft velvet peak at front and tied velvet bow on top. Labelled *Henderson's, Liverpool*, about 1965-73.

WAG 2001.45.155 Group of nine hat trimmings and artificial flowers, including roses and bunches of violets, about 1930s-50s.

WAG 2001.45.156 Group of long tail feathers from the Greater Bird of Paradise, one of the seven species of the genus *Paradisaea*, all of them found on New Guinea and the neighbouring islands, used for trimming hats, about 1920-40.

WAG 2001.45.157 Box of ostrich feathers, brown, black and white, used for trimming hats. Labelled *Owen Owen Ltd, London Road, Liverpool, Mrs P.F. Tinne, Clayton Lodge, Aigburth, Date 24/9/24*, 1924.

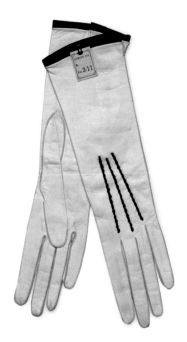

9. ACCESSORIES AND JEWELLERY

1967.187.234b Pair of women's stockings, knitted blue silk, with paler blue line and 'clock' running up outside of leg, about 1850-70.

1967.187.235 Pair of women's stockings, knitted white silk, knitted woollen tops, about 1920-30s.

1967.187.236 Pair of women's stockings, knitted brown cotton, lacy openwork pattern reaching halfway up leg, about 1900-20.

1967.187.237 Pair of women's stockings, knitted cotton, purple and white horizontal stripes with purple line and 'clock' running up outside of leg. Labelled *D.E.T.*, about 1880-1900. Belonged to Emily Tinne's mother-in-law, Deborah E. Tinne (1856-1923).

1967.187.464 Pair of women's stockings, knitted coffee-coloured silk, lisle tops, heels and toes, stitched back seams. Stamped *Pure Silk, 260 Spring Needle* and labelled *Slimtex Pure Silk, Seal of Satisfaction*, about 1920-35. Cat. no. 207.

1967.187.465 Pair of women's stockings, knitted ochre-coloured silk, lisle tops and feet, stitched back seams and embroidered 'clocks'. Labelled *8/11, Sand, 100, 5943*, about 1920-35. Cat. no. 208.

1967.187.466 Pair of women's stockings, knitted brown silk, lisle tops, heels and toes, stitched back seams. Stamped *Spring needle knit, Pure silk panel, Made in England* and labelled *Invicta, Shapex ankle, made from best quality pure silk with lisle tops and feet, British Made* and *Invicta, Regd., Shapex, British Made*, about 1920-35. Cat. no. 206.

1967.187.503a-d Four identical pairs of men's spats, natural-coloured linen, lined with white cotton twill, side-fastening with four mother-of-pearl buttons, linen strap and buckle for beneath foot, about 1880-1900. Probably belonged to Philip Tinne's uncle, Herman William Tinne (1853-1937) and are stored in 1967.187.500, his top hat case.

1967.187.238 Pair of women's gloves, dark brown kid leather, machine-embroidered decoration to backs and cuffs in black and red silk. Stamped *Real kid, F, made in Belgium*, about 1920-30. Cat. no. 187.

1967.187.239 Pair of women's gloves, dark brown kid leather, machine-embroidered decoration to cuffs in lilac and white silk. Stamped *Real kid, made in Belgium*, about 1920-30.

1967.187.240 Pair of women's gloves, white kid leather, machine-embroidered decoration to backs and cuffs in black and white silk. Stamped *Real kid, F, made in Belgium*, about 1920-30.

1967.187.241 Pair of women's gloves, white kid leather, machine-embroidered decoration to backs and cuffs in brown and white silk. Stamped *Real kid, F, made in Belgium*, about 1920-30. Cat. no. 186.

1967.187.242 Pair of women's gloves, white kid leather edged with black leather, black silk embroidery to backs, elasticated gusset at wrists. Stamped *Real kid, made in Belgium* and labelled *Lewis's Ltd, Price 3/11*, about 1920-30. Cat. no. 188.

1967.187.243 Pair of women's gloves, white kid leather, black cotton embroidery to backs, black leather gores with white machine-embroidery. Stamped *Made in Italy*, about 1928-34.

1967.187.244 Pair of women's gauntlet-style gloves, white kid leather, black cotton embroidery to backs, black leather gores with white machine-embroidery. Stamped *Made in Italy* and labelled *2/-* (crossed out) and *1/9*, about 1928-34. Cat. no. 190.

1967.187.245 Pair of women's gauntlet-style gloves, white kid leather, black cotton embroidery to backs, scalloped black leather gores. Labelled *2/11* (crossed out) and *2/-*, about 1928-35. Cat. no. 191.

1967.187.246 Pair of women's gauntlet-style gloves, cream-coloured knitted rayon silk, black and white rayon embroidery to backs, black and white rayon silk cord piping to scalloped wrists. Labelled *Artificial silk, Made in Germany* and *2/9*, about 1930-34. Cat. no. 192.

1967.187.247 Pair of women's gauntlet-style gloves, dusty pink knitted rayon silk, paler pink rayon gores and piping to edges. Stamped *Artificial Silk, Made in England* and *Fournes Own Make*, and labelled *3/11*, about 1930-35. Cat. no. 196.

1967.187.248 Pair of women's evening gloves, beige-coloured knitted cotton, mother-of-pearl buttons at wrist, about 1920-30. Cat. no. 198.

1967.187.249 Pair of women's evening gloves, beige-coloured knitted cotton, mother-of-pearl buttons at wrists, about 1920-30. Cat. no. 199.

WAG 2001.45.128 Pair of women's gauntlets, brown fake fur, brown leather palms. Labelled *Pinkham Gloves, Made in England* and *Wool and cotton gloves, Leather palms, made in England*, about 1930-35.

WAG 2001.45.129 Pair of women's gauntlet-style gloves, brown suede, cuffs trimmed with dyed brown rabbit fur, lined with pale grey wool. Labelled *7, English Make*, about 1930-35. Cat. no. 197.

WAG 2001.45.130 Woman's single glove, black leather, trimmed with dyed black rabbit fur, lined with white rabbit fur. Labelled *7, English Make*, about 1930-35.

WAG 2001.45.131 Pair of women's gloves, white chamois leather, fingers sewn with contrasting black cotton thread. Stamped *Washable* and *Leather gloves, Made in England*, about 1930-35. Cat. no. 193.

WAG 2001.45.132 Pair of women's gloves, white chamois leather, elasticated gussets at wrists, stamped *Velve, Washable*, about 1928-34.

WAG 2001.45.133 Pair of women's gloves, white chamois leather, fastening with two mother-of-pearl buttons at wrists, about 1928-35.

WAG 2001.45.134 Pair of women's gloves, white chamois leather, fastening with two mother-of-pearl buttons at wrists. Original washing instructions printed on card inside one glove, about 1928-35.

WAG 2001.45.135 Pair of women's gloves, white chamois leather. Original washing instructions printed on card inside one glove, about 1928-35. Cat. no. 189.

WAG 2001.45.136 Pair of women's gloves, white chamois leather, elasticated gussets at wrists, stamped *Velve, Washable*, about 1928-34.

WAG 2001.45.137 Pair of women's gloves, white chamois leather, elasticated gussets at wrists, stamped *Velve, Washable* and labelled *Lewis's Ltd, price 3/9*, about 1928-34.

WAG 2001.45.138 Pair of women's gloves, white kid leather edged with black leather, black silk embroidery to backs, elasticated gussets at wrists. Stamped *Made in Germany*, about 1920-30.

WAG 2001.45.139 Pair of women's gloves, white kid leather edged with pale tan-coloured leather, brown silk embroidery to backs, elasticated gussets at wrists. Stamped *Made in Belgium*, about 1920-30.

WAG 2001.45.140 Pair of women's gauntlet-style gloves, beige-coloured chamois leather, running stitch around fingers. Stamped *English Make, Washable*, about 1928-35. Cat. no. 194.

WAG 2001.45.141 Pair of women's gloves, light tan-coloured chamois leather, elasticated gussets at wrists, stamped *Washable*, about 1928-34.

WAG 2001.45.142 Pair of women's gloves, light tan-coloured chamois leather, elasticated gussets at wrists, stamped *Washable*, about 1928-34.

WAG 2001.45.143 Pair of women's gloves, light tan-coloured chamois leather, elasticated gussets at wrists, stamped *Washable*, about 1928-34.

WAG 2001.45.144 Pair of women's gloves, light tan-coloured chamois leather, elasticated gussets at wrists, stamped *Washable*, about 1928-34.

WAG 2001.45.145 Pair of women's gauntlet-style gloves, tan-coloured antelope suede, plaited suede edging to cuff. Stamped *Real antelope, English Make, Washable* and labelled *Lewis's Ltd, Price 10/6*, about 1930-35. Cat. no. 195.

1967.187.389 Jabot, white cotton net, cotton muslin centre, machine-made lace edging, about 1910-20. Cat. no. 203.

1967.187.390 Jabot, white cotton net, black moiré silk bow at top, mother-of-pearl buttons, machine-made lace edging, about 1910-20.

1967.187.391 Jabot, cream-coloured silk crepe, black moiré silk ribbon, mother-of-pearl buttons, machine-made lace edging. Labelled *Bon Marché (Liverpool) Ltd*, about 1915-25. Cat. no. 204.

1967.187.392 Jabot, starched white cotton muslin, cut on diagonal at bottom edge, machine-made lace edging, about 1910-20. Cat. no. 202.

1967.187.393 Jabot, cream-coloured silk crepe, black moiré silk bow at top, machine-made lace inserts and edging, about 1910-20.

1967.187.394 Jabot, ivory-coloured silk crepe, black moiré silk bow at top, machine-made lace edging, about 1915-25. Cat. no. 201.

1967.187.395 Jabot, cream-coloured silk crepe, machine-made lace insert and edging, about 1910-20.

1967.187.396 Jabot, white starched and pleated cotton muslin, machine-made lace edging, black silk ball-buttons, about 1920-30. Cat. no. 205.

1967.187.397 Jabot, cream-coloured machine-knitted wool, turtle neckline and ruffled front section. In original box, marked *The "Diana", Knitted Jabot, Pat. No.9653 of 1912* and *Made in Germany*, 1912. Cat. no. 200.

1967.187.398 Woman's collar, cream-coloured silk crepe, deep border of machine-made lace, embroidered with leaf pattern in pale blue silk, about 1910-20.

1967.187.399 Woman's collar, cream-coloured silk crepe, fine vertical pin-tucks, machine-made lace edging, about 1910-20.

1967.187.400 Woman's collar, cream-coloured silk, fine vertical pin-tucks, machine-made lace edging, about 1910-20.

1967.187.401 Woman's collar, cream-coloured silk chiffon, machine-made lace insert and deep border. Labelled 5/11 (crossed out) 2/11?, about 1910-20.

1967.187.402 Woman's collar, cream-coloured machine-made lace, worked in a scrolling pattern, about 1910-20.

1967.187.403 Woman's collar, cream-coloured silk crepe de chine, three rows of pin-tucks, cotton machine-lace edging. Labelled 3/6?, 4/6? (crossed out), about 1910-20.

1967.187.404 Woman's collar, cream-coloured crocheted cotton, about 1910-20.

1967.187.474 Headdress, dyed black egret feathers, the tips left white, wired together on circular frame, elastic at centre back, about 1920-30. Cat. no. 209.

1967.187.475 Headdress, black celluloid strips and sequins, mounted on stiff cotton tiara-shaped base, about 1920-30. Cat. no. 210.

1967.187.476 Hair ornament, dyed black curled egret feathers, secured at base with cotton thread, about 1920-30. Cat. no. 211.

1967.187.336 False hairpiece, auburn-coloured human hair, covered with fine brown silk net, on domed, oval-shaped framework. Labelled Good Goods Brand, Reg.no.590 575, No........, Price, Gold Medallist and Highest Award, London, 1906, about 1905-15. Cat. no. 214.

1967.187.337 False hairpiece, auburn-coloured human hair, covered with fine black silk net, on domed, oval-shaped framework, about 1905-15. Cat. no. 215.

1967.187.338 False hairpiece, auburn-coloured human hair, on domed, circular-shaped framework, about 1905-15. Cat. no. 212.

1967.187.339 False hairpiece, auburn-coloured human hair, on long oval-shaped support of woven horsehair, about 1905-15. Cat. no. 213.

1967.187.424 Lorgnette, tortoiseshell frame, long flat handle with rounded end and loop for chain, about 1900.

1967.187.425 Lorgnette, tortoiseshell frame and short, squared-off handle with loop and copper ring at end, about 1900.

1967.187.426 Necklace, the 'rope' composed of alternating coiled silver wire and diamanté pastes, pendant composed of two wing shapes of pale grey pearlised plastic. Labelled Bon Marché, Liverpool, Made in France, 35/-, about 1925-30. Cat. no. 216.

1967.187.427a & b Necklace and dress clip, the necklace composed of plaited, gilt-metal braids, the daisy-shaped pendant of pale pink pearlised plastic with decorative gilt-metal centre. Matching dress clip, about 1925-35. Cat. no. 218.

1967.187.428a & b Necklace and pair of dress clips, the necklace composed of plaited gilt-metal braids, the daisy-shaped pendant of pale blue pearlised plastic with decorative gilt-metal centre. Pair of matching dress clips, about 1925-35. Cat. no. 217.

1967.187.429 Necklace, five rows of pale pink rolled cotton organza, held together with silvered metal mounts, central rose-head pendant of pale pink plastic, about 1920-40.

1967.187.430 Necklace, five rows of pale blue rolled cotton organza, held together with silvered metal mounts. Labelled 3/6, about 1920-40.

1967.187.477 Choker-necklace, narrow black silk moiré ribbon, central section made of three squares of woven black and silver steel beads, about 1920-30.

1967.187.431 Hatpin, steel, the silver head in the shape of a golf club, maker's mark K & T, Birmingham assay mark for 1906. Cat. no. 229.

1967.187.432 Hatpin, steel, with curled silver head set with a small coral stone, Chester assay mark for 1906. Cat. no. 224.

1967.187.433 Pair of hatpins, steel, the silver button-shaped tops of amber-coloured enamel over an engine-turned ground, inscribed B.J.D. April 2nd 1910, Birmingham assay mark for 1909. Cat. no. 219.

1967.187.434 Hatpin, steel, silver head in the form of an open flower, maker's mark P & T, Birmingham assay mark for 1917. Cat. no. 222.

1967.187.435 Pair of hatpins, steel, base metal heads in the form of long ears of wheat, set with amber-coloured glass beads, about 1900-10. Cat. no. 226.

1967.187.436 Hatpin, steel, silvered base metal head, a filigree dome set with blue glass pastes, about 1900-10. Cat. no. 220.

1967.187.437 Pair of hatpins, steel, small stylised floral heads of silver filigree and wirework, set with silver beads, about 1900-10. Cat. no. 223.

1967.187.438 Hatpin, steel, ball-shaped silver filigree head, about 1900-10. Cat. no. 225.

1967.187.439 Hatpin, steel, inverted teardrop-shaped mother-of-pearl head, set into silver mount with silver bead on top, about 1900-15. Cat. no. 228.

1967.187.440 Four hatpins, steel, all with black glass bead-shaped heads, about 1900-20. Cat. no. 221.

1967.187.441 Hatpin, steel, the head a large piece of mother-of-pearl shell with silver wire coiled around it, about 1900-10. Cat. no. 227.

10. BABIES' AND CHILDREN'S CLOTHES

1967.187.125 Young girl's dress, navy blue wool gabardine, long plain sleeves, turned-over linen collar with hand-embroidered design in blue and yellow silk, about 1921-24. Probably worn by Elspeth Tinne (1911-2000). Cat. no. 261.

1967.187.126 Young girl's party dress, white cotton lawn, low waistline with narrow black velvet ribbon, seven rows of flounces to skirt, hand-embroidered in orange, blue, black and yellow silk, about 1920-25. Cat. no. 256.

1967.187.127 Young girl's party dress, pale blue cotton organdie, ruffles to neckline, cuffs and skirt, with dusty pink velvet ribbon and two bows to waistline, about 1917-18. Cat. no. 255.

1967.187.128 Young girl's party dress, eau-de-nil coloured cotton organdie, ruffles to neckline, cuffs and skirt, ribbon decoration now missing from waistline, about 1916-20.

1967.187.129 Young girl's dress, cream wool cashmere, smocking to yoke, waist and cuffs, about 1915-20.

1967.187.130 Toddler's dress, white cotton lawn, torchon bobbin lace trimming and broderie anglaise insertions, about 1913-20. Cat. no. 250.

1967.187.131 Young girl's dress, ivory-coloured rayon silk, decorated with smocking, about 1920-30. Cat. no. 252.

1967.187.132 Baby's short dress, white cotton lawn, trimmed with broderie anglaise, about 1911-20s. Cat. no. 243.

1967.187.133 Young girl's dress, white cotton lawn, bodice and skirt decorated with broderie anglaise, about 1917-18.

1967.187.134 Toddler's dress, white cotton, the Peter Pan collar, bodice front and waistline all embroidered with scrolling design in royal blue cotton, about 1914. Worn by Elspeth Tinne (1911-2000) aged about 3. Cat. no. 251.

1967.187.135 Young girl's dress, white cotton, decorated with broderie anglaise trim or inserts, about 1915-20.

1967.187.136 Baby's short dress, white cotton lawn, trimmed with Valenciennes lace, about 1911-20s. Cat. no. 245.

1967.187.137 Young girl's dress, white cotton lawn, decorated with broderie anglaise, trimmed with Bedfordshire-type machine-made lace, about 1920.

1967.187.138 Toddler's dress, white cotton, decorated with broderie anglaise, trimmed with torchon lace, about 1920-25.

1967.187.139 Baby's short dress, white cotton, decorated with broderie anglaise, trimmed with torchon lace, about 1915-20.

1967.187.140 Young girl's dress, white cotton lawn, decorated with broderie anglaise, trimmed with Bedfordshire-type machine-made lace, about 1916-20.

1967.187.141 Baby's short dress, white cotton muslin, trimmed with broderie anglaise and machine-made lace, about 1912-20.

1967.187.142 Young girl's dress, gold/orange knitted silk, scalloped hem, about 1920-25.

1967.187.143 Young girl's dress, white cotton organdie, the sleeve-edgings, turned-down collar, edges of bodice front and low waistband all of mid-blue cotton organdie, with panel of drawn threadwork to bodice front. Labelled *14*, about 1924-26. Probably worn by Elspeth Tinne (1911-2000). Cat. no. 262.

1967.187.144 Young girl's dress, white cotton organdie, low waistline, with panel of drawn threadwork to bodice front. Labelled *14*, about 1924-26. Probably worn by Elspeth Tinne (1911-2000).

1967.187.145 Young girl's smock dress, pale blue cotton denim, the yoke, turned-down collar and cuffs all edged with blanket stitch in white wool. Labelled *E.M. Tinne*, about 1921-23.

1967.187.146 Young girl's smock dress, pale blue cotton denim, the seams of the bodice decorated with white woollen running stitch, the turned-down collar embroidered with floral motif in white wool. Embroidered *Tinne*, about 1921-23. Cat. no. 258.

1967.187.147 Young girl's smock dress, pale blue denim cotton, the yoke, collar and cuffs embroidered with floral motifs in white silk, about 1921-23.

1967.187.148 Young girl's dress, natural-coloured tussah silk, the bodice front and cuffs smocked and embroidered with brown silk, the turned-down collar embroidered with circular motifs in brown silk chain stitch, about 1918-19. Worn by Elspeth Tinne (1911-2000) aged about 7-8, and then by Bertha Tinne (1916-75) aged about 10. Cat. no. 260.

1967.187.149 Young girl's dress, natural-coloured tussah silk, the yoke and cuffs smocked and embroidered with brown silk, the turned-down collar embroidered with brown silk border and motifs, about 1918-19. Probably worn by Elspeth Tinne (1911-2000) aged about 7-8. Cat. no. 257.

1967.187.150 Young girl's dress, pink cotton, sleeveless, the V-shaped neckline and turn-over collar edged with white cotton, about 1925.

1967.187.151 Young girl's gymslip, navy blue wool serge, fastening on the shoulders with two buttons, three box pleats falling from the yoke at front and back. Labelled *24*, about 1916-17.

1967.187.152 Toddler's coat, cream wool, lined with white cotton, double-breasted, six large mother-of-pearl buttons, about 1915-20s. Cat. no. 273.

1967.187.153 Young child's coat, cream wool serge, lined with white cotton sateen, double-breasted, large mother-of-pearl buttons, about 1915-20s.

1967.187.154 Toddler's coat, cream wool cashmere, lined with white cotton sateen, four decorative mother-of-pearl buttons, deep collar with broderie anglaise inserts and frill. Labelled *6271*, about 1913-14. Worn by Elspeth Tinne (1911-2000) aged about 2-3. Cat. no. 270.

1967.187.155 Toddler's coat, cream wool cashmere, lined with white cotton sateen, single-breasted, the lower section cut in knife pleats, four decorative mother-of-pearl buttons. Labelled *523* and *T2344*, about 1915-20s.

1967.187.156 Toddler's coat, cream wool cashmere, lined with white cotton sateen, single-breasted, five mother-of-pearl buttons, about 1915-20s. Cat. no. 272.

1967.187.157 Young child's coat, white cotton poplin, double-breasted, six large mother-of-pearl buttons, about 1916-20s.

1967.187.157a Toddler's coat, white cotton poplin, double-breasted, six large mother-of-pearl buttons, about 1915-20s. Cat. no. 274.

1967.187.158 Toddler's coat, white sprigged cotton muslin, single-breasted, six mother-of-pearl buttons, about 1913-20s. Cat. no. 271.

1967.187.159 Baby's coat, white cotton poplin, single-breasted, two small mother-of-pearl buttons, about 1915-20s. Cat. no. 269.

1967.187.160 Baby's coat, cream corded silk, lined with cream Jap silk, two silk satin ribbon ties at neckline, about 1911-20s. Cat. no. 267.

1967.187.161 Baby's coat, cream wool cashmere, lined with white cotton sateen, fastens at neckline only, about 1911-20s.

1967.187.162 Baby's coat, cream wool cashmere, lined with white cotton sateen, fastens at neckline only, about 1911-20s.

1967.187.163 Baby's coat, cream wool cashmere, lined with cream Jap silk, double-breasted, mother-of-pearl buttons, about 1911-20s.

1967.187.164 Baby's coat, cream silk and alpaca, lined with white linen, fastens at neckline only, about 1911-20s.

1967.187.165 Young boy's sailor jacket, white cotton, fly-front fastening concealing the buttons, sailor collar, about 1915-20s.

1967.187.166 Young boy's sailor jacket, white cotton drill, fly-front fastening concealing the linen-covered buttons, white sailor collar. Labelled *G.H.Lee & Co.Ltd, Basnett Street, Liverpool*, about 1918. Probably worn by John Ernest Tinne (1913-96). Cat. no. 264.

1967.187.167a & b Young boy's sailor suit, blue and white striped cotton, a jacket and matching shorts, fly-front fastening to the jacket concealing linen-covered buttons. Labelled *G.H.Lee & Co.Ltd, Basnett Street, Liverpool*, about 1918-20. Probably worn by John Ernest Tinne (1913-96). Cat. no. 265.

1967.187.168a & b Young girl's middy blouse, navy blue wool serge, and matching skirt, fly-front fastening to the blouse concealing buttons, the sailor collar and edge of skirt both decorated with applied bands of narrow woollen braid. Blouse labelled *Specialite "Lancaster" Costume, LP Co.*, about 1916-17. Probably belonged to Elspeth Tinne (1911-2000). Cat. no. 263.

1967.187.169 Young girl's middy blouse, navy blue wool serge, the fly-front fastening concealing the buttons, a crowned, crossed anchor motif and three stripes embroidered in gold silk thread on the upper left sleeve. Labelled *Hope Bothers Ltd, 44-46 Ludgate Hill, London E.C.*, about 1916-17. Probably belonged to Elspeth Tinne (1911-2000) aged about 5-6. Cat. no. 263.

1967.187.170 Young boy's Eton suit, jacket, waistcoat and trousers, black wool, the jacket lined with quilted black cotton sateen, the waistcoat lined with blue and grey striped cotton, the trousers with white pinstripe and turn-ups. Jacket labelled *John Walls Ltd, Eton College, J.E. Tinne Esq*, the waistcoat and trousers labelled *John Walls Ltd, 13 & 14 High Street, Eton, Tel. Windsor 292 (Chitty's), J.E. Tinne Esqire*, about 1927-28. Belonged to John Ernest Tinne (1913-96) who attended Eton between 1927 and 1931.

1967.187.171 Young girl's nightdress, white cotton, full-length, the collar and cuffs edged with broderie anglaise, inscribed *E.D.Tinne* in ink, about 1916-17. Belonged to Elspeth Tinne (1911-2000).

1967.187.172 Young girl's nightdress, white cotton, full-length, the collar and cuffs edged with broderie anglaise, inscribed *E.D.Tinne* in ink, about 1916-17 Belonged to Elspeth Tinne (1911-2000). Cat. no. 239.

1967.187.173 Young girl's nightdress, white cotton, full-length, the collar and cuffs edged with broderie anglaise, inscribed *E.D.Tinne* in ink, about 1916-17. Belonged to Elspeth Tinne (1911-2000).

1967.187.174 Young girl's nightdress, white cotton, full-length, the collar and cuffs edged with broderie anglaise, inscribed *E.D.Tinne* in ink, about 1916-17. Belonged to Elspeth Tinne (1911-2000).

1967.187.175 Young girl's nightdress, white cotton, full-length, the collar and front placket edged with broderie anglaise, labelled *E.M.Tinne*, about 1916-17. Probably belonged to Elspeth Tinne (1911-2000).

1967.187.176 Pair of young girl's drawers, white cotton, narrow band of drawn threadwork at each knee and cotton ruffle trimmed with torchon bobbin lace, labelled *Sterling, £, Lock Stitch, Trade Mark, S & S*, made by Stapley and Smith of London Wall, about 1913-20s. Cat. no. 236.

1967.187.177 Pair of young girl's drawers, white cotton, whitework embroidery to legs, about 1913-20s.

1967.187.178 Pair of young girl's drawers, cream-coloured wool, white cotton waistband, torchon lace trim to legs, about 1913-20s.

1967.187.179 Young girl's bodice, cream-coloured cotton twill, lacing up centre back, eight bone buttons to centre front, boned down the back, elasticated cotton suspenders. Labelled *The S & S Comforto Bodice*, made by Stapley and Smith of London Wall, about 1915-20s. Cat. no. 237.

1967.187.180 Young girl's petticoat, cream-coloured wool flannel, sleeveless, fastening down centre back with two linen-covered buttons, about 1913-20s.

1967.187.180a, b & c Three baby's bibs, white cotton twill, V-shaped, fastening on right shoulder with two linen-covered buttons and at waist with loops and ties. Labelled *Elspeth D. Tinne*, about 1911-12. Belonged to Elspeth Tinne (1911-2000).

1967.187.181a & b Two baby's bibs, cream wool serge backed with white linen, V-shaped, fastening on right shoulder with two linen-covered buttons and at the waist with loops and ties, about 1911-12. Probably belonged to Elspeth Tinne (1911-2000).

1967.187.182a, b & c Three children's sailor collars, white cotton, with buttonholes at back of necks and on shoulders for attachment to shirt or jacket, about 1915-20.

1967.187.183a, b & c Three baby's sailor collars, white linen backed with white cotton, with navy blue silk feather embroidery all around edges. Labelled *Elspeth D. Tinne*, about 1911-12. Belonged to Elspeth Tinne (1911-2000).

1967.187.184a, b, c, d, e, g, h Seven young boy's sailor collars, navy blue cotton, three backed with white cotton, four backed with navy blue cotton, all decorated with three narrow applied white cotton bands, sewn close together, about 1918-20. Probably worn by John Ernest Tinne (1913-96) with a sailor jacket. Cat. no. 264.

1967.187.185a, b, c, e, f, **h, i** Seven young boy's sailor cuffs, navy blue cotton, two of them backed with white cotton, five backed with navy blue cotton, all decorated with three narrow applied white cotton bands, sewn close together, about 1918-20. Probably worn by John Ernest Tinne (1913-96) with a sailor jacket. Cat. no.264.

1967.187.186 Baby's collar, white cotton muslin, with padded cotton under-collar, embroidered with floral whitework motifs. Piece of muslin attached horizontally at bottom, with slots for coloured ribbon. Labelled *Owen Owen Ltd, Liverpool, 1/6?*, about 1911-20s. Cat. no. 279.

1967.187.186a Baby's collar, white cotton muslin, with padded cotton under-collar, embroidered with floral whitework motifs, Valenciennes lace inserts, labelled *E.M. Tinne*, about 1911-20s. Cat. no. 276.

1967.187.186b Baby's collar, white cotton muslin, with padded cotton under-collar, embroidered with floral whitework motifs, about 1911-20s. Cat. no. 278.

1967.187.186c Baby's collar, white cotton piqué, with under-collar of white cotton twill, embroidered all over with white dots in circles and triangles, about 1911-20s. Cat. no. 277.

1967.187.187 Pair of girl's stockings, machine-knitted brown cotton, stamped *British Make* on the feet and labelled *2/11*, about 1925-35.

1967.187.188 Pair of girl's stockings, machine-knitted brown cotton. Labelled *2/11*, about 1925-35.

1967.187.189 Pair of girl's stockings, machine-knitted brown cotton, stamped *Everlast Hosiery, Combed Egyptian Lisle Cotton, Made in England*, on the feet, about 1925-35.

1967.187.190 Pair of girl's stockings, machine-knitted brown wool, stamped *Silean, Pure wool, Made in England, High spliced ankle, Double soul, Special wide tops*, on the feet, and labelled *Owen Owen, Liverpool, 3/11*, about 1925-35.

1967.187.191 Three pairs of girl's stockings, machine-knitted black wool, stamped *Two fold Botany Wool, three fold ankle & foot, for school and gym wear, made in England, Size 8, CC41, K712, 1592* on the foot, Utility, about 1941-45.

1967.187.192 Pair of girl's stockings, machine-knitted black wool, stamped *All wool, Made in England*, and labelled *Lewis's Ltd, Liverpool, No.5, Price 1/6*, about 1935-45. Cat. no. 281.

1967.187.193 Pair of girl's stockings, machine-knitted black wool, stamped *Spliced knee, ankle, heel & foot*, on the foot, and labelled *W.H.Watts & Co. Ltd, Liverpool* and *4/11 ribs, Diamond knees, perfect fitting, all wearing parts are extra spliced, fast dye, special finish*, about 1935-45. Cat. no. 280.

1967.187.194 Pair of girl's stockings, machine-knitted black wool, stamped *All wool, Made in England* on the foot, and labelled *Lewis's Ltd, Liverpool, Price 1/6*, about 1935-45.

1967.187.195 Pair of girl's stockings, machine-knitted grey cotton, stamped *'Dixone', Holeproof, Made in England* at the tops, about 1935-45.

1967.187.196 Pair of young child's ankle socks, machine-knitted navy blue and white striped cotton, about 1920-40.

1967.187.197a Pair of baby's bootees, pale blue kid leather, lined with white cotton sateen, fastening up outer side with three tiny mother-of-pearl buttons, about 1914-20s.

1967.187.197b Pair of baby's socks, machine-knitted pale blue silk, with decorative pattern, about 1920-40.

1967.187.198 Pair of baby's shoes, black leather, lined with natural-coloured linen canvas, fastening with ankle strap and button, about 1911-20s.

1967.187.199 Pair of young child's shoes, white buckskin, leather soles and heels, strap across instep fastening with white glass button, stamped *Peter Pan, Regd,* about 1915-20s.

1967.187.200 Pair of young child's shoes, white cotton canvas, leather soles and heels, fastening with two small white boot-buttons on the vamps, stamped *Bally's, Swiss Manufacture.* In original shoe box, labelled *Button shoes, white, Bally, Manufactured in Switzerland*, about 1915-30s. Cat. no. 283.

1967.187.201 Pair of young child's shoes, white cotton canvas, leather soles and heels, fastening at sides with two boot-buttons, about 1915-20s.

1967.187.202 Pair of young child's gloves, cream-coloured mercerised cotton with ribbed cuffs, about 1920-40.

1967.187.203 Pair of child's sock driers, white glazed earthenware, in the form of two hollow feet, to ankle level, stamped *Wedgwood, 3CO*, the factory's date-code for 1907-24. Cat. no. 282.

1967.187.208 Child's sailor hat, navy blue wool, lined with gold cotton sateen, bound with navy blue silk ribbon embroidered with *H.M.S.Tiger* in gold letters. Labelled *6 7/8*, about 1918-20s.

1967.187.209 Child's cap, dark blue wool, lined with black cotton, with standing band, labelled *J.Ernest Tinne*, about 1918-20.

1967.187.210 Bodice from doll's dress, the skirt now detached and missing, dark brown cotton velvet, lined with natural-coloured linen, decorated with brass studs and applied glass beads, about 1900-20s.

1967.187.211 Child's fancy dress jester's jacket, red and yellow cotton 'motley', with hood and deep pointed-edged collar trimmed with bells. Coxcomb and two points on hood, with bells attached. Pointed edges to over-sleeves and bottom edge also trimmed with bells, about 1918-20s.

1967.187.212 Doll, pink knitted body, blue glass eyes, painted features, yellow velvet jacket and cap. Marked *Chad Valley, Hygienic Toys*, made by Chad Valley, Birmingham, about 1930-40.

1967.187.213 Pair of young child's boots, white suede, squared toes, low heels, fastening up the sides with buttons, about 1915-20s.

1967.187.214 Pair of child's ankle socks, machine-knitted white cotton with pale blue horizontal stripes, about 1915-20s.

1967.187.469 Pair of young child's combinations, cream-coloured machine-knitted wool, front-fastening, open underneath, labelled *Reform, C.B., Guaranteed Quality*, with sheep's head logo. Made by Charles Bayer of London Wall, about 1918-20s. Cat. no. 238.

1967.187.470 Young child's bathing costume, navy blue machine-knitted cotton jersey, fastening on left shoulder with two buttons, with bands of red and white striped jersey at neckline, armholes and legholes, about 1920-30. Cat. no. 266.

1967.187.495a Baby's cot curtain, white cotton muslin with tiny spot motif and stripe, lined with pale blue glazed cotton, about 1911-30.

1967.187.495b Baby's cot valance, white cotton muslin with tiny spot motif and stripe, deep double flounce edged with machine-made lace, about 1911-30.

1967.187.495c Baby's cot cover, white cotton muslin with tiny spot motif and stripe, lined with pale blue glazed cotton, about 1911-30.

1967.187.495d Baby's cot pillow cover, white cotton muslin with tiny spot motif and stripe, backed with pale blue glazed cotton, about 1911-30.

1967.187.495e Baby's basket, for accessories (?), centre filled with cotton wool padding covered with white cotton muslin with tiny spot motif and stripe, lined with pale blue cotton. Four handles covered with pale blue silk ribbon, machine-made lace trimming. Made as part of baby's layette (?), about 1911-30.

1967.187.505 Young boy's coat, brown wool, double-breasted, blue and gold cotton sateen half-lining, labelled *Alwetha Raincoats, Regd.*, about 1935. Probably belonged to Philip (Pip) Tinne (1929-95) aged about 5. Cat. no. 275.

1967.187.508 Doll's pram, wooden frame, the hood and body of black American cloth, lined with black and green leatherette. Woven basket attached to curved handle by two leather straps, about 1935-40.

1967.187.509 Pair of young girl's gaiters, brown leather lined with brown wool felt, fastening down outer side with ten small boot buttons, leather strap and metal buckle beneath instep. Labelled *Peter Pan, Regd. No. 290908*, about 1920-40.

WAG 2001.45.68 Young girl's dress, white cotton muslin, short puffed sleeves, white-work embroidery to bodice ruffle and hemline, about 1838. Belonged to Philip Tinne's great aunt, Alexandrina Petronella Francine Tinne (b.1835), explorer of the Sudan, who was killed by Tuareg tribesman in 1969.

WAG 2001.45.69 Young girl's petticoat, white cotton muslin, sleeveless, floral whitework embroidery to the ruffle at the hemline, about 1838. Worn with WAG 2001.45.68, above.

WAG 2001.45.70 Toddler's dress, ivory silk, the bodice front and cuffs decorated with smocking, about 1913. Possibly belonged to Elspeth Tinne (1911-2000) aged about 2.

WAG 2001.45.71 Baby's coat, cream-coloured silk, double-breasted, with wide pleats to centre front, deep collar with broderie anglaise flounce, the buttons now missing, about 1911-12. Belonged to Elspeth Tinne (1911-2000). Cat. no. 268.

WAG 2001.45.72 Baby's bonnet, ivory silk satin, trimmed with machine-made lace and silk ribbon rosette, with satin ribbon ties, about 1911-12. Belonged to Elspeth Tinne (1911-2000).

WAG 2001.45.73 Original photograph of Elspeth Tinne (1911-2000), aged about 2-3, seated on chair in garden, wearing cream wool cashmere coat, **1967.187.154**, and a bonnet, about 1913-14

WAG 2001.45.74 Original photograph of Elspeth Tinne (1911-2000), aged about 2-3, lying on rug in garden, wearing cream wool cashmere coat, **1967.187.154**, and a bonnet, about 1913-14.

WAG 2001.45.75 Young girl's dress, white cotton lawn, bands of whitework embroidery and machine-made lace, about 1915-16. Belonged to Elspeth Tinne (1911-2000), aged about 4-5. Cat. no. 254.

WAG 2001.45.76 Toddler's dress, white cotton muslin, short sleeves, low waistline marked by muslin belt tying at centre back, crocheted trim to sleeves and hemline. Labelled 6, about 1926. Probably worn by Alexine Tinne (1923-2011), aged about 3. Cat. no. 253.

WAG 2001.45.77 Baby's dress, white cotton lawn, broderie anglaise and machine-made lace insertions, about 1911-20s. Cat. no. 244.

WAG 2001.45.78 Baby's dress, white cotton, inserted bands of whitework braid with 'buttonhole' feature, broderie anglaise flounce to hemline, about 1911-20s.

WAG 2001.45.79 Baby's dress, white cotton lawn, inserted rows of Bedfordshire bobbin lace, pin-tucks and whitework embroidery, about 1911-20s.

WAG 2001.45.80 Toddler's dress, white cotton lawn, whitework-embroidered leaves with cutwork petals down centre front, faggoting at hemline and around armholes, about 1925-26. Probably belonged to Alexine Tinne (1923-2011).

WAG 2001.45.81 Baby's dress, white cotton lawn, whitework embroidery and cutwork eyelets, about 1920-30.

WAG 2001.45.82 Baby's dress, white cotton lawn, whitework embroidery and faggoting, about 1911-20s.

WAG 2001.45.83 Baby's dress, white cotton lawn, cutwork eyelets, embroidered cutwork flowerheads, crocheted cotton border to hemline, about 1920-30.

WAG 2001.45.84 Baby's dress, white cotton lawn, bodice decorated with embroidered whitework wreath at centre front, about 1920-30.

WAG 2001.45.85 Baby's dress, white cotton lawn, embroidered whitework dots in a chevron pattern, and machine-made Valenciennes lace inserts, about 1911-20s.

WAG 2001.45.86 Baby's dress, ivory silk crepe de chine, short puffed sleeves, vertical pin-tucks and machine-made Valenciennes lace inserts worked with four leaf clovers, about 1920-30. Cat. no. 246.

WAG 2001.45.87 Baby's dress, white silk crepe covered with layer of machine-embroidered net, short puffed sleeves, about 1920-30. Cat. no. 247.

WAG 2001.45.88 Baby's long christening gown, white cotton lawn, decorated all over with floral whitework embroidery, swags and bows and cutwork butterflies, about 1911. Worn by most of the Tinne children for their christenings at St Anne's Church, Aigburth, Liverpool, 1911-29. Cat. no. 240.

WAG 2001.45.89 Baby's long gown, white cotton, short sleeves, deep inverted V-shaped section to centre front, with alternating pin-tucks, bands of inserted broderie anglaise and whitework embroidery. Labelled E.M. Tinne, about 1911-20s.

WAG 2001.45.90 Baby's long gown, white cotton, short sleeves, the bodice of whitework embroidery and broderie anglaise. Labelled E.M. Tinne, about 1911-20s.

WAG 2001.45.91 Baby's long gown, white cotton, decorated with alternating pin-tucks and inserted bands of broderie anglaise. Labelled E.M. Tinne, about 1911-20s. Cat. no. 241.

WAG 2001.45.92 Baby's long gown, white cotton lawn, with alternating pin-tucks and inserted bands of whitework embroidery to bodice, inserted bands of machine-made Bedfordshire lace to skirt, about 1911-20s. Cat. no. 242.

WAG 2001.45.93 Baby's long gown, white cotton lawn, vertical pin-tucks and machine-made Valenciennes lace insertions, about 1911-20s.

WAG 2001.45.94 Baby's long petticoat, white cotton, trimmed with torchon bobbin lace. Labelled E.M. Tinne, about 1911-20s. Cat. no. 232.

WAG 2001.45.95 Baby's long petticoat, white cotton, pin-tucks, whitework embroidery and scalloped border of broderie anglaise. Labelled E.M. Tinne, about 1911-20s.

WAG 2001.45.96 Baby's long petticoat, cream-coloured brushed cotton, wrap-over flaps and tapes to centre back, embroidered with cream-coloured silk, about 1911-20s. Cat. no. 233.

WAG 2001.45.97 Baby's long petticoat, cream-coloured brushed cotton, wrap-over flaps and tapes to centre back, embroidered with cream-coloured silk, about 1911-20s.

WAG 2001.45.98 Baby's short petticoat, white cotton, sleeveless, the neckline, armholes and hem all scalloped and embroidered over, about 1913-20s. Cat. no. 234.

WAG 2001.45.99 Toddler's petticoat, white cotton, drawn threadwork at bodice front and hemline, with dagged and embroidered edge, about 1925. May have belonged to Alexine Tinne (1923-2011), aged about 2. Cat. no. 235.

WAG 2001.45.100 Baby's blouse, white cotton lawn, fastening at neckline with single tiny mother-of-pearl button, the collar, cuffs and bottom of front edges all decorated with embroidered floral cutwork, about 1920-30. Cat. no. 248.

WAG 2001.45.101 Baby's cardigan, white hand-knitted wool, long wide sleeves, no fastenings, about 1911-20s. Cat. no. 249.

WAG 2001.45.102, 103,104,105,106, 107 Six babies' vests, white cotton lawn, all decorated around necklines and armholes with applied machine-made lace, about 1911-20s. Cat. no. 231.

WAG 2001.45.108, 109, 110, 111, 112, 113, 114 Seven babies' binders, white cotton, each with five cotton tapes sewn at each end, for tying around baby. One still has original strip of wool flannel with it, worn beneath for warmth, about 1911-20s. Cat. no. 230.

WAG 2001.45.115 Baby's bonnet, ivory silk covered with layer of needlerun net, applied silk ribbon and rosettes, two ties of needlerun net, about 1911-20s.

WAG 2001.45.116 Baby's bonnet, needlerun net, the original silk lining now removed, applied pale green silk ribbon and rosettes, two ties of needlerun net, about 1911-20s.

WAG 2001.45.117 Baby's bonnet, ivory silk covered with layer of needlerun net, applied ivory silk ribbon, one ribbon tie of spotted ivory silk, about 1911-20s.

WAG 2001.45.118 Baby's bonnet, ivory silk covered with layer of needlerun net, applied machine-made lace and ivory silk ribbon, bunch of artificial forget-me-nots at each side, two ties of needlerun net, about 1911-20s.

WAG 2001.45.119 Baby's bonnet, ivory silk, lined with ivory silk, applied machine-made lace, ribbon rosettes and silk braid, two long broad ties of ivory silk, about 1915-20s.

WAG 2001.45.120 Baby's bonnet, white cotton lawn, deep turned-back brim with broderie anglaise edging and whitework embroidery, two ties of pale blue silk, about 1911-20s.

WAG 2001.45.121 Baby's bonnet, ivory silk satin, lined with ivory silk, decorated with machine-made Bedfordshire lace, rosettes and embroidery on the crown, two long ties of ivory silk satin, about 1911-12. Probably belonged to Elspeth Tinne (1911-2000).

WAG 2001.45.122 Deep band of sky-blue silk, possibly a sash from a child's dress, about 1915-20s.

WAG 2001.45.123 Baby's cot cover, cream wool cashmere, with scalloped edges, applied floral motifs in the corners and at edges in embroidered ivory silk, about 1911-20s.

WAG 2001.45.124 Baby's collar, white cotton, in two layers, the upper layer decorated with whitework embroidery, labelled E.M. Tinne, about 1911-20s.

WAG 2001.45.125 Baby's collar, white cotton, in two layers, the upper layer decorated with whitework embroidery, labelled E.M. Tinne, about 1911-20s.

WAG 2003.11.5 Young girl's dress, brown hand-knitted wool, short sleeves, squared neckline, bands of crocheted wool to neckline, sleeves and scallop-edged hem. Knitted drawstring cord through waistline, ending in two woollen pom-poms, about 1923-25. Possibly the same dress worn by Bertha Tinne (1916-75) in a family photograph, aged about 8 years. Cat. no. 259.

WAG 2003.11.6 Young girl's dress, brown hand-knitted wool, three quarter-length sleeves, crocheted edge to neckline, sleeves and hemline, about 1924-26.

WAG 2003.11.7 Young girl's dress, brown hand-knitted wool, three quarter-length sleeves, crocheted edge to neckline, sleeves and hemline, about 1924-26.

SERVANTS' CLOTHES

1967.187.206 Servant's cap, white cotton, gathered around the head into turned-back brim, labelled E.M. Tinne, about 1920-40.

1967.187.207 Servant's cap, white glazed cotton, gathered around the head into turned-back brim. Labelled Brewsters, 53 & 55 Byrom Street, Liverpool, about 1920-40.

1967.187.406 Woman's overall, or house smock, green cotton, wrap-around ties at centre front, smocking detail beneath yoke, about 1920-30.

1967.187.408 Waist apron, white cotton muslin, floral whitework embroidery and machine-made lace trim to centre front, about 1910-20.

1967.187.409a Cook's apron, starched white linen, square bib cut all in one with skirt, labelled Brewsters, 53 & 55 Byrom Street, Liverpool, about 1920-40.

1967.187.409b Cook's apron, starched white linen, square bib cut all in one with skirt, labelled Brewsters, 53 & 55 Byrom Street, Liverpool, about 1920-40.

1967.187.409c Cook's apron, starched white linen, square bib cut all in one with skirt, about 1920-40.

1967.187.410a Maid's afternoon apron, cap, collar and pair of cuffs, starched white cotton muslin, all with faggoting decoration, the cap with applied narrow band of black cotton velvet. Labelled 015, 1111, about 1920-40.

1967.187.410b Maid's afternoon apron, cap, collar and pair of cuffs, starched white cotton muslin, all with faggoting decoration, the cap with applied narrow band of black cotton velvet. Labelled 015, 1/11, Dept 23, Art 147, about 1920-40.

1967.187.410c Maid's afternoon apron, cap, collar and pair of cuffs, starched white cotton muslin, all with faggoting decoration, the cap with applied narrow band of black cotton velvet. Labelled 015, 1/11, about 1920-40.

1967.187.410d Maid's afternoon apron, cap, collar and pair of cuffs, starched white cotton muslin, all with faggoting decoration, the cap with applied narrow band of black cotton velvet, about 1920-40.

1967.187.411 Maid's afternoon apron, starched white cotton muslin, square-shaped bib, black cotton velvet belt at waistband, labelled J22, 1/6?, about 1920-40.

1967.187.412 Maid's afternoon apron, starched white cotton muslin, square-shaped bib, whitework embroidery and drawn threadwork, labelled K13, 1/3?, about 1920-40.

1967.187.413 Maid's afternoon apron, starched white cotton, square-shaped bib, whitework embroidery. Labelled K13, 1/6?, about 1920-40.

1967.187.414 Maid's afternoon apron, starched white cotton muslin, three wide vertical pleats to centre front of bib and skirt. Labelled L11, 1/6?, about 1920-40.

1967.187.415 Maid's afternoon apron, starched white cotton muslin, whitework embroidery, about 1920-40.

1967.187.416 Maid's afternoon apron, starched white cotton, machine-made drawn threadwork, about 1920-40.

1967.187.417 Maid's afternoon apron, starched white cotton muslin, three appliquéd white cotton butterflies, labelled K17, 1/3?, about 1920-40.

1967.187.418a Maid's collar and pair of cuffs, starched white cotton, whitework embroidered braid, about 1920-40.

1967.187.418b Maid's collar and pair of cuffs, starched white cotton, whitework embroidered braid, labelled Price 1/-, R/MM, about 1920-40.

1967.187.418c Maid's collar and pair of cuffs, starched white cotton, whitework embroidered braid, labelled Price 1/-, R/MM, about 1920-40.

1967.187.419 Maid's cap, starched white cotton, with band of black cotton velvet at centre front, about 1920-40.

1967.187.420 Maid's cap, starched white cotton, with narrowly pleated cotton frill, narrow band of black cotton velvet secured at centre front by leaf-shaped appliquéd whitework motif. Labelled K13, 6/-, about 1920-40.

1967.187.421 Maid's afternoon cap, starched white cotton muslin crimped into narrow vertical pleats, narrow black cotton velvet ribbon to centre front. Labelled No.525, Price 1/6, about 1920-40.

1967.187.422 Apron, white cotton, edging of broderie anglaise, three narrow, horizontal pin-tucks to skirt. Labelled E.M. Tinne and L8. 8422, about 1920-40.

1967.187.423 Apron, white cotton, square-shaped bib with insert and edging of broderie anglaise. Labelled E.M. Tinne and L8. 8422, about 1920-40.

12. HOUSEHOLD FURNISHINGS

1967.187.462 Tablecloth? Curtain?, cream-coloured cotton, the two outer edges woven with narrow band of red elephants on a yellow ground, possibly Indian, about 1920-40.

1967.187.463 Hot water bottle cover, cream-coloured wool, the top, bottom and right-hand side left unsewn. Embroidered Hot Water on front in two shades of green wool, about 1930-40.

1967.187.496 Tablecloth or table runner, white cotton damask, woven all over with small diamond motif and at each end with a band of Greek key pattern. Faggoting detail to each end. Embroidered H.M.T. and labelled E.M. Tinne, about 1910-40.

1967.187.497 Valance from chair or dressing table?, white cotton damask, large-scale pattern of flowers and leaves, with cotton tape ties at each end and centre for securing to piece of furniture, about 1900-30.

1967.187.498a & b Pair of curtains, white cotton muslin, with slotted headings and drawstring tapes, small machine-embroidered spot motif and larger looped bows. Muslin frill along one long side and bottom of each curtain, about 1900-30.

1967.187.499a-c, Three curtains, white cotton muslin, with small machine-embroidered spot motifs and larger fleurs-de-lys motifs, two of them with drawstring tapes through the headings, one with the drawstring missing, about 1900-30.

13. MISCELLANEOUS

1967.187.446 Fabric length, dark chocolate brown silk crepe, about 1920-40.

1967.187.447 Fabric length, turquoise blue and grey cotton and rayon mix, brocaded in a stylised leaf pattern, about 1930-40.

1967.187.448 Fabric length, black silk, printed with design of white curves and squares, about 1920-40.

1967.187.449 Fabric length, black silk, figured all over with circles of flower heads linked by meandering lines on a spotted ground, about 1920-40.

1967.187.450 Fabric length, dark blue silk velvet with printed design of bamboo leaves in brown and white, on small floral spot-motif ground, about 1930-40.

1967.187.451 Fabric length, black silk velvet, labelled Made in Italy, about 1920-40.

1967.187.452 Fabric length, claret-coloured silk velvet, about 1920-40.

1967.187.453 Fabric length, deep blue silk velvet, about 1920-40.

1967.187.454 Fabric length, dark brown silk velvet, about 1920-40.

1967.187.455 Fabric length, royal blue silk velvet, about 1920-40.

1967.187.456 Fabric length, purple-blue silk velvet devoré, with waving diaper-like design, about 1920-40.

1967.187.457 Fabric length, aubergine-coloured silk velvet, about 1920-40.

1967.187.458 Fabric length, purple crushed silk velvet, about 1920-40

1967.187.459 Fabric length, black silk velvet, with woven copper-coloured silk backing, labelled 3, 21/-, about 1920-40.

1967.187.460 Fabric length, claret-coloured crushed silk velvet, about 1920-40.

1967.187.461 Fabric length, purple silk velvet, about 1920-40

WAG 2001.45.126 Woman's headband, pink silk satin, formed from two rosettes linked by a ruched band, decorated with ribbon rose buds, secured with length of elastic tape. Labelled 3/11 (crossed out) and 1/6, about 1920-25.

WAG 2001.45.127 Safety pin 'tidy', pale blue silk satin ribbon in form of bow attached to central plastic ring with four hanging ribbons, each ending in smaller plastic rings. Safety pins of various sizes attached to all four rings, about 1920-30s.

WAG 2001.45.158 Fabric length, Macclesfield silk, red, cream, beige and black stripes, about 1930-35. Bought by Emily Tinne to make summer dresses for her young daughters.

WAG 2001.45.159 Fabric length, Macclesfield silk, pink, blue, cream and aubergine-coloured stripes, about 1930-35. Bought by Emily Tinne to make summer dresses for her young daughters.

WAG 2001.45.160 Fabric length, Macclesfield silk, red, yellow, blue, pink, green and cream stripes, about 1930-35. Bought by Emily Tinne to make summer dresses for her young daughters.

WAG 2003.11.12 Copy of The Art Annual for 1897, the life and work of William Q. Orchardson, R.A., 1897.

WAG 2003.11.13 Copy of Weldon's Bazaar of Children's Fashions, including paper patterns for a child's dress and dolls' clothes, September 1914.

WAG 2003.11.14 Copy of Leach's Lady's Companion, 22 May 1915.

WAG 2003.11.15 Copy of Harrison's Dressmaker, including paper pattern for blouse, October 1916.

WAG 2003.11.16 Copy of Bestway Novelty Jumpers, about 1918-20.

WAG 2003.11.17 Copy of Weldon's Jumpers, Knitting and Crochet, about 1920-23.

WAG 2003.11.18 Copy of Bestway Outsize Summer Fashions, with paper pattern for afternoon dress, about 1929-31.

WAG 2003.11.19 Copy of Weldon's Smart Fashions for Outsizes, including two paper patterns for dresses, about 1930.

WAG 2003.11.20 Copy of Weldon's Ladies' Journal, Portfolio of Fashions, including paper patterns for dresses and coats, 1934.

WAG 2003.11.21 Copy of Weldon's Outsize Fashions, including paper patterns for dress and coat, about 1932-34.

WAG 2003.11.22 Copy of Weldon's Smart Fashions for Wider Hips, including three paper patterns for dresses, about 1932-34.

WAG 2003.11.23 Copy of Weldon's Matrons, including paper patterns for two dresses and coat, 1936.

WAG 2003.11.24 Copy of Weldon's Matrons' Winter Styles, including paper patterns for two dresses and coat, 1936.

WAG 2003.11.25 Copy of Weldon's Outsize Coats and Frocks, including paper patterns for two dresses and coat, 1936.

WAG 2003.11.26 Copy of Excella patterns, November 1935.

WAG 2003.11.27 Copy of Butterick Fashion News, November 1935.

WAG 2003.11.28 Copy of Weldon's Outsize Underwear, including paper patterns for two nightdresses and a petticoat, about 1935.

WAG 2003.11.29 Copy of Weldon's Semi-Evening Styles for Outsizes, including two paper patterns for dresses, about 1935.

WAG 2003.11.30 Copy of Weldon's Smart Outsizes, including paper patterns for two dresses and coat, 1936.

WAG 2003.11.31 Copy of Art & Craft Education, August 1937.

WAG 2003.11.32 Fold-out advertising leaflet for men's and women's swimwear, from Jantzen, the man's shop, ground floor, George Henry Lee & Co. Ltd, Basnett Street, Liverpool, 1939.

WAG 2003.11.33 Paper pattern for infant's long coat, in original packet, The Aspinall Practical Paper Patterns, about 1900-15.

GLOSSARY

Abalone shell – The shell of a marine snail found in most warm seas, especially the Pacific Ocean. It is used to decorate a variety of objects, jewellery and dress accessories.

Alpaca – A soft fabric woven from the hair of the alpaca, a member of the camel family native to Peru. Alpaca hair is often mixed with silk or wool.

American cloth – Also known as oil cloth, a cotton fabric with a linseed oil-based finish on one side, glazed to make it waterproof.

Appliqué – Any fabric or other decorative motif applied to the ground of another fabric by sewing or embroidering, to form a pattern or design.

Bertha collar – A deep collar on a woman's dress or bodice, sometimes extending over the shoulders, often made of lace or decorated net.

Boat neckline – A wide, horizontally cut neckline on a woman's dress or bodice, without a collar.

Bolero – A short, fitted jacket without front fastenings, worn over a dress or bodice, and often made in a matching fabric.

Bias-cut – A garment cut out on a diagonal line to the *warp* and *weft* threads of a fabric, in order to make it drape well and cling closely to the contours of the wearer's body. Especially popular for underwear, day and evening dresses during the 1930s.

Broderie anglaise – A form of embroidery, developed from the 1820s onwards, in which a decorative pattern is cut into a white cotton ground and the edges are then over-stitched with white cotton thread.

Bugle – A small, tubular glass bead, used extensively in the decoration of garments from the late nineteenth century until the 1930s.

Busk – A stiffener for the centre-front of a corset, usually made of wood, steel or whalebone and often sewn into the garment.

Bust bodice – A forerunner of the brassière, worn around 1900-1910, to cover the breasts rather than shape or support them. Usually made of cotton with very light boning and fastening down the centre-front to waist level.

Camisole – An under-bodice, usually of fine cotton, worn with drawers beneath the corset during the nineteenth and early twentieth centuries.

Celluloid – A semi-synthetic and highly flammable form of early plastic. Used from the 1870s onwards for jewellery and dress accessories.

Chain stitch – An embroidery stitch composed of interlocking chains, worked either with a needle or hook. Sometimes referred to as *tambour work*, especially when embroidered on to a fine cotton ground.

Chinoiserie – A western European style, originating in the seventeenth century, imitating Chinese art forms and including features such as Chinese pagodas, landscapes and figures. It can be found across all of the decorative arts, including dress and textiles.

Cloche – A type of close-fitting hat, often of wool felt or fine straw, popular during the late 1920s and early 1930s. It takes its name from the French term for the glass, bell-shaped cover used to protect young plants from frost and resembles it in shape.

Clock – An embroidered line of silk, often topped with a small decorative motif, running up the outside of a stocking from the ankle.

Coatee – A woman's softly fitted jacket with centre-front fastening, made to match an evening or dinner dress, especially during the late 1920s and 1930s.

Combinations – A one-piece item of underwear, combining the *camisole* and the drawers, originally developed for women during the 1870s. It fastened down the centre-front and underneath, usually with linen-covered buttons.

Cotton – The soft, fluffy fibre produced by the seed pod of the cotton plant. It can be woven alone or mixed with many other fibres to produce a wide range of fabrics.

> **brushed** – a cotton with soft, raised surface fibres, produced by combing or brushing with wire brushes.
> **denim** – a smooth-surfaced, hardwearing cotton, usually dyed in various shades of indigo blue and used for jeans. Can also be found in lighter weights and colours for other garments.
> **drill** – a hardwearing, coarse cotton fabric often used for uniforms.
> **glazed** – a cotton with a wax or starch applied to its surface to give a slightly shiny finish.
> **lawn** – a finely woven, sheer cotton fabric, often used for women's garments and babies' and children's clothes.
> **mercerised** – cotton yarn treated with caustic soda to give it a stronger, softer and silkier finish. Named after its creator, John Mercer, who developed the process in 1844.
> **muslin** – a soft, lightweight cotton with a plain, open weave.
> **organdie** – a lightweight, transparent cotton fabric with a slightly starched finish.
> **piqué** – a textured cotton fabric, woven with a surface pattern resembling a honeycomb.
> **poplin** – a lightweight, finely woven cotton with a fine rib effect.
> **sateen** – a smooth-surfaced fabric produced by weaving with a cotton *warp* and a silk or *rayon weft*. The resulting fabric resembles the more expensive silk *satin* but is harder wearing.

Cowl neckline – A softly draped neckline at the front or back of a woman's dress, named after the term for a monk's hood.

Cravat – A term used from the 1660s onwards, mainly to describe a man's neckcloth, usually made of fine linen, tied in a number of decorative ways. Also used to describe a short fur neck tie for women, especially during the 1930s.

Crepe – A term used to describe fabrics with a crinkled surface, usually produced by weaving with a twisted thread. Crepes can be made from natural fibres like silk and wool and from synthetics like *rayon*.

Crin – The French term for horsehair, used during the nineteenth century as a braided stiffener for petticoats. During the 1920s and 1930s it was used extensively in hat-making for crowns and brims.

Crochet – Cotton and woollen thread or yarn looped into a design using a crochet hook. Used for decorative borders and inserts in textiles and garments.

Cuban heel – A block-shaped heel, built up from several layers of leather, popular for women's shoes during the 1930s.

Cutwork – A needlework technique in which part of the ground fabric is cut away and the resulting spaces then filled with a number of decorative stitches.

Dagged – Ornamental cutting or pointing of the edge of a garment, often a sleeve or a hemline.

Damask – A reversible fabric with a design worked partly in a *satin* weave and partly in a plain weave, resulting in contrasting shiny and matt areas. Damask can be made in a range of fibres, including silk, cotton, linen, *rayon* and wool.

Diamanté – A colourless glass paste used for making inexpensive costume jewellery and dress accessories in imitation of diamonds.

Drawn threadwork – A needlework technique in which threads are pulled or drawn out of a ground fabric and the remaining threads are sewn over using a number of different stitches to produce a decorative effect or pattern.

Duster coat – A woman's loosely cut coat, often with wide, three-quarter length sleeves and without front fastenings. Popular during the 1920s together with matching dresses.

Engageantes –The French term for a detachable under-sleeve, usually of lace or fine cotton *muslin,* loosely stitched to the sleeve lining. They could be easily removed for washing or when the fashion changed.

Engine-turned – Mechanically incised decoration of a ceramic or metal surface using an electric lathe.

Espadrilles – A canvas shoe with plaited or braided rope or cord sole, originally worn in Spain, parts of France and Italy. Adopted in Britain for seaside and holiday wear during the late nineteenth century.

Facing – A separate piece of fabric, sewn to the underside of collars, cuffs and *revers* in order to give a neat finish.

Faggotting – A decorative technique in which threads are pulled out from a fabric and some of the remaining cross threads are tied together in the middle.

Feathers

    egret – a small heron-like bird, found in many tropical and sub-tropical areas of the world, whose pure white feathers, often dyed, were used extensively in hat-making during the nineteenth and twentieth centuries.

    marabou – a large African stork. The short, fluffy feathers from its tail and wings were used as a trimming for luxury garments.

Feather stitch – A looped embroidery stitch often used during the late nineteenth and early twentieth centuries to decorate women's and children's underwear and nightwear.

Figured – See *Silk, brocade.*

Filigree – Metal decoration, usually made from very slender threads of gold or silver and occasionally base metals. Used in jewellery-making since ancient times.

Fly fastening / fly front – A fastening in which the buttons, buttonholes or zip are concealed beneath a strip of fabric.

French knots – A twisted, knotted embroidery stitch, often worked randomly across areas of open ground in a design.

Fur

    angora rabbit – a long, silky fur, used for trimming garments or mixed with other fibres and woven into fabric.

    chinchilla – a very soft, grey fur from a small rodent native to South America.

    ermine – the winter coat of the weasel, pure white, often decorated with small black tails.

    mink – the dark brown fur of a member of the weasel family.

    nutria – the dense under-fur of the coypu, a large rodent found in South America.

    Persian lamb – the curly fur of young lambs bred in Persia, Russia and Afghanistan, often dyed black.

    sable – the dark brown, almost black, fur of the marten, a member of the weasel family.

    silver fox – a long, dark, silky fox fur, the top layer of hairs tipped with white, giving a silvery effect.

Gauze – A lightweight, transparent fabric, made of silk, cotton or *rayon*.

Godet – See *gore.*

Gore – A triangular piece of fabric inserted between two other pieces in a garment, often at the sides of a skirt, to give greater width. Sometimes referred to as a *godet.*

Gusset – A triangular piece of fabric inserted between two other pieces in a garment, often beneath the arms or between the legs, to give extra width and allow for greater ease of movement by the wearer.

Herringbone weave – A weave made in two different directions, like a zig-zag, and looking like the bones found in a herring.

Jabot – A detachable ruffle of fine cotton, linen or lace worn at the neck and falling down the centre front of a dress or bodice.

Jersey – A stretchy, machine-knitted fabric made from wool, cotton, *rayon*, silk or a mixture of fibres.

Jute – A material made from the stem fibres of two plants (*Corchorus capsularis* and *Corchorus olitorius*) found mainly in China and the Indian sub-Continent, especially Pakistan. A coarse fabric, used for backing carpets and making twine, bags and sacks, it can also be mixed with other fibres like silk and wool.

Lace – A decorative trimming or insert for garments, composed of a network of linen, cotton or silk threads and made either by hand with a needle or by twisting the threads attached to bobbins, or later by a number of machine techniques.

> **Bedfordshire** – A medium-weight, open-patterned bobbin lace, made in the English Midlands, often combining geometric and floral designs.
> **blonde** – Lace made from silk thread, rather than linen or cotton.
> **tape** – A bobbin lace made in a long, continuous narrow length, arranged and sewn down in various patterns.
> **torchon** – A coarse bobbin lace of cotton or linen thread, made to a simple design.
> **Valenciennes** – A lightweight, densely patterned bobbin lace, often used during the late nineteenth and early twentieth centuries to trim women's underwear and babies' clothes.

Leather

> **chamois** – the strong, stretchy skin of the chamois goat, usually a deep yellow in colour but sometimes paler.
> **glacé kid** – goatskin with a smooth, shiny surface finish, often used for gloves and shoes.
> **patent** – a lacquered leather with a highly polished surface, used for shoes and handbags.

Linen – A fabric made from the woven fibres of the flax plant. It can be made in a range of weights, from very light and sheer to heavy and coarse.

Lisle – A twisted cotton thread used in the machine knitting of women's stockings during the 1920s, 30s and 40s. They often have a shiny appearance when worn.

Louis heel – A low, waisted heel shape, popular for women's shoes during the 1920s, and named after those worn by King Louis XV of France during the eighteenth century.

Mantle – A woman's loose cape or wrap, usually waist-length and sleeveless, sometimes with a hood.

Mother-of-pearl – A general term for the hard inner lining of certain marine mollusc shells, including oysters and mussels. Colours vary from pale grey, pink and blue to green, depending on the origin of the shell. Used for small decorative objects, jewellery and dress accessories.

Needlerun net – A decorated net, made to imitate lace, produced by darning or embroidering a pattern on to a net ground, initially by hand and later by machine.

Open-leg drawers – Women's drawers consisting of two separate legs joined only at the waistband and not sewn together underneath to form a crotch.

Pagoda sleeve – An elbow or three quarter-length sleeve in a woman's dress or bodice, often cut into a number of flounces and increasing in size down the arm. Named after the Chinese pagoda, or temple building whose flared-out roof it resembles in shape.

Petersham ribbon – A narrow, ribbed fabric woven from cotton or silk and used as stiffening or for decoration in garments and hats.

Pin-tuck – A narrow fold of fabric in part of a garment, stitched into place to form a decorative effect. Often used during the nineteenth and early twentieth centuries on women's and children's underwear and women's blouses.

Placket – The fold of fabric in a skirt, bodice or pair of trousers into which the fastenings, including buttons, zips and hooks, are sewn and concealed.

Pleats – a number of folds made in a fabric for decoration or to control volume.

> **accordion** – narrow pleats resembling the folds in the bellows of an accordion.
> **box** – pleats arranged to point alternatively left and right, producing a box-like fold between them.
> **knife** – sharply folded pleats, all pointing in the same direction.

Quarter – The side of a shoe, stretching from the *vamp* to the heel.

Quilted – Two layers of fabric, often with a layer of wool sandwiched between them for warmth, sewn together using geometric or other decorative stitching.

Raffia – A strong, shiny straw made from the leafstalks of the raffia palm tree, grown in Madagascar. It was used mainly for making or decorating hats, bags and baskets.

Rayon – A shiny, synthetic fabric made from cellulose, a substance derived from wood-pulp and treated with caustic soda to produce a liquid known as viscose. This can be spun into a thread and woven on its own or mixed with many other fibres to produce a wide range of fabrics.

Rever – The turned-back section at the front opening of a jacket or coat, combining the collar and lapels.

Rick rack braid – A narrow, woven cotton or silk braid made in a wavy, zigzag pattern.

Rouleau, plural **rouleaux** – The French term for a narrow roll of fabric or ribbon used as trimming on garments, especially on collars.

Running stitch – The most basic, simple stitch, formed by passing the needle in and out of a fabric so that the stitches run one in front of the other.

Satin – A type of weave in which the closely packed *warp* threads completely cover the *weft* threads, giving the resulting fabric a smooth, shiny surface finish. Early satins were always made from silk but later versions were made from cotton, *rayon* and a mixture of other fibres.

Scalloped – A decorative, semi-circular edge cut into a garment, resembling the edge of a scallop shell.

Shattering – The term used to describe the disintegration and flaking away into pieces of tin-weighted silk, often used to line women's bodices and skirts during the late nineteenth and early twentieth centuries. The silk was immersed in a preparation of metal salts during production, to make it glossy, but deteriorates badly after long exposure to pollutants in the atmosphere.

Shawl collar – A long, turned-over collar, resembling the drape of a shawl around the neckline.

Silk – The smooth, continuous fibre spun from the cocoon of the silk worm. It can be woven alone or mixed with many other fibres to produce a wide range of fabrics.

    brocade – a luxurious silk fabric, usually of floral motifs in contrasting colours, often on a *satin* weave ground. The design, formed by the addition of extra *weft* threads, is slightly raised on the surface but 'floats' across the reverse of the fabric. Sometimes referred to as *figured* silk.

    chiffon – a very fine, transluscent, plain woven silk.

    corded – any fabric, especially silk, which has a ribbed surface produced as part of the weave.

    crepe-de-chine – a lightweight, plain woven silk made with a plain *warp* thread and a twisted *weft* thread.

    faille – a plain woven silk fabric with a finely ribbed surface.

    georgette – a lightweight, plain woven silk fabric with a slightly *crepe* effect, produced by using twisted *warp* and *weft* threads.

    Jap – a lightweight, plain woven silk fabric, very smooth and soft to the touch and often used for garment linings. Also known as *Habutai* silk.

    moiré – a ribbed silk fabric which has been heated and machine-rolled to flatten the ribs in an uneven, rippling pattern. The resulting finish often resembles a water stain, giving the fabric its alternative name, *watered* silk.

    ottoman – a heavily ribbed or corded silk fabric, sometimes woven with wool in the *weft* to produce a fuller, more rounded rib effect.

    shantung – see *tussah*.

    shot – a plain woven silk made from different coloured *warp* and *weft* threads. The resulting fabric catches the light in contrasting directions, giving it an iridescent effect.

    tussah – a coarse-textured silk made from the cocoons of wild rather than cultivated silkmoths. Its natural colour is yellow-brown and it is often left undyed. Tussah silk is used to make *shantung*, another coarse silk fabric with an uneven surface finish.

Slip – A woman's one-piece undergarment, like a simple petticoat, often fitted to the figure, especially during the 1930s. Also, the term for the toe-piece of a shoe, applied in a separate, often decorative leather.

Smocked – A needlework technique in which the fullness of a garment is gathered together into narrow pleats or tubes and held in place by means of decorative stitches.

Sprigged – A fabric decorated with small randomly sewn or embroidered floral motifs.

Taffeta – A crisp, lightweight, finely ribbed fabric, usually of silk or *rayon*, that makes a rustling sound when worn.

Tambour – see *chain stitch*.

Turtle neckline – A raised, knitted neckline in a woollen or *jersey* garment.

Twill – A strong, diagonally woven fabric in wool, cotton or silk.

Vamp – The front part of a shoe, including the toe.

Velour – A soft wool or silk fabric with a dense surface texture, produced in a similar way to *wool facecloth*. Often used for women's coats and hats during the 1920s and 30s.

Velvet – A soft, luxurious silk or cotton fabric woven with a raised, cut pile surface.

    devoré – a technique in which a velvet ground fabric is printed with a chemical to burn away part of the surface, leaving a contrasting, sheer pattern.

    panne – a type of velvet in which the long pile has been flattened down in one direction by mechanical rollers, producing a shiny, decorative surface.

Voile – A sheer, lightweight fabric, usually made of cotton but sometimes of silk or wool, and often used for women's underwear and blouses.

Warp – The vertical threads in any piece of woven fabric, crossed by the *weft* threads which run over and under them.

Warp-printed – A technique in which the *warp* threads of a fabric are printed with a design before being woven. When the plain-coloured *weft* threads are woven in it produces a blurred effect in the finished fabric.

Weft – The horizontal threads in any piece of woven fabric, running over and under the vertical *warp* threads.

Whitework – Embroidery done in white cotton thread, usually on to a white cotton ground, in a wide variety of stitches.

Wool – The hair of the sheep, which can be woven alone or mixed with many other fibres to produce a wide range of fabrics.

    cashmere – the hair of the Himalayan goat, found in Kashmir (from which it takes its name) China, Tibet and parts of the Middle East. Often mixed with wool to produce a fine, soft woven or knitted fabric.

    facecloth – a fine, smooth wool in which the surface, or face of the fabric, has been raised by brushing to produce a nap. This nap is then beaten back down, leaving a dense, weather-resistant finish to the cloth.

    flannel – a soft, loosely woven woollen fabric with a raised surface texture or nap, often used to line garments or for women's petticoats due to its warmth and absorbancy.

    gabardine – a hardwearing fabric often woven from worsted wool, the long fibres of the sheep's fleece which have been combed to lie smoothly next to each other as spun yarn. Gabardine's dense, diagonal weave makes it water-resistant and ideal for outdoor garments such as raincoats.

    nun's veiling – a lightweight, plain woven woollen fabric, with a slightly crinkled surface finish similar to *crepe*. Used originally for religious garments and later for garment linings.

    serge – a hardwearing, slightly coarse fabric, usually woven from worsted wool, the long fibres of the sheep's fleece which have been combed to lie smoothly next to each other as spun yarn. Serge was often used for uniforms and outdoor garments due to its hardwearing qualities.

SELECT BIBLIOGRAPHY

Adburgham, Alice, *Shops and Shopping, 1800-1914,* George Allen & Unwin, London, 1964

Battersby, Martin, *Art Deco Fashion, French Designers 1908-1925,* Academy Editions, London, 1974

Blum, Stella, ed., *Everyday Fashions of the Twenties as Pictured in Sears and Other Catalogs,* Dover Publications, Inc., New York, 1981

Briggs, Asa, *Friends of the People, The Centenary History of Lewis's,* Batsford, London, 1956

de la Haye, Amy, Taylor, Lou, and Thompson, Eleanor, *A Family of Fashion, The Messels: Six Generations of Dress,* Philip Wilson Publishers and Brighton Museum & Art Gallery, London, 2005

Dorner, Jane, *Fashion in the Twenties and Thirties,* Ian Allan, London, 1973

Garland, Madge, Ginsberg Madeleine, Battersby, Martin, Lloyd, Valerie and Davies, Ivor, *Fashion 1900-1939,* A Scottish Arts Council Exhibition with the support of the Victoria and Albert Museum, Idea Books International, London, 1975

Ginsburg, Madeleine, *Paris Fashions, The Art Deco Style of the 1920s,* Bracken Books, London, 1989

Hall, Carolyn, *The Thirties in Vogue,* Harmony Books, New York, 1985

Kjellberg, Anne and North, Susan, *Style and Splendour, the Wardrobe of Queen Maud of Norway 1896-1938,* V & A Publications, London, 2005

Lancaster, Bill, *The Department Store, A Social History,* Leicester University Press, London, 1995

Owen, Elizabeth, *Fashion in Photographs 1920-1940,* Batsford and the National Portrait Gallery, London, 1993

Reynolds, Helen, *Couture or Trade, An Early Pictorial Record of the London College of Fashion,* Phillimore, Chichester, 1997

Rolley, Katrina and Aish, Caroline, *Fashion in Photographs 1900-1920,* Batsford and the National Portrait Gallery, London, 1992